Fathers and Sons

Fathers and Sons

Essays by Todd Richissin · Photographs by Jim Graham

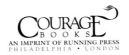

COURAGE BOOKS
AN IMPRINT OF RUNNING PRESS
PHILADELPHIA · LONDON

Photographs © 2000 by Jim Graham
Text © 2000 by Todd Richissin
All rights reserved under the Pan-American and
International Copyright Conventions
Printed in China

9   8   7   6   5   4   3   2
Digit on the right indicates the number of this printing

Library of Congress Cataloging-in-Publication Number 99-75090

ISBN 0-7624-1536-3

Designed by Frances J. Soo Ping Chow
Edited by Marc E. Frey
B&W Film: Agfa SCALA 200x Professional Black & White 35mm Slide Film
Cameras: Canon EOS-1n cameras/Canon EF USM lenses
Lighting: Lowel DP Lights (tungsten)
Kodak Pro Photo CD Scans: Quaker Photo, Philadelphia
Typography: ITC Berkeley Old Style

This book may be ordered by mail from the publisher.
Please include $2.50 for postage and handling.
But try your bookstore first!

Running Press Book Publishers
125 South Twenty-second Street
Philadelphia, Pennsylvania 19103-4399

Visit us on the web!
www.runningpress.com

There are too many fathers in this world who believe caring for their sons is an option rather than an obligation.

This book is dedicated to my father and all the other fathers who have given a damn.

—TPR

To my mother, Bernadine Marie for being both a loving mother and father during a time when single parenting was uncommon. To my father, James J. Graham, and stepfather, Robert Sherlock Holmes, and to all of the fathers and sons in our book who help me appreciate my father's love even more.

—JG

We would also like to dedicate this book to Adam Petty, Henry Graves and Asher Zagar, all good men, who agreed before their passing to be a part of our book. We have chosen to leave their chapters as originally written so that, as we did, you can admire and experience the extraordinary relationships they shared as fathers and sons.

—Richissin and Graham

Contents

Acknowledgments

My most sincere thanks to my editor at Running Press, Marc Frey, who counseled, criticized, and praised with uncommon good humor and whose deft editing touch I value almost as much as the friendship that developed; to Brian Perrin, who had faith that I could tackle such a book; to Brooke Cain, my researcher, who tolerated my organizational laxness with understanding, a laugh, and plenty of backup files; to Steve Leicher at Steve's Travel in Cleveland who somehow got me where I needed to go, always with an eye toward getting me there for happy hour and, if not, at least for last call. Special thanks to Cam, Dan, Julie, Jane, Emily, Jason, Paul, Ellen, Tom, Thomas, the Boys from Brook Park and Garrett, old friends and new, who knew all varieties of circumstances I faced during the writing of this book and never once were at a loss for patience and encouraging words. Very special thanks to my brothers, who (usually) showed me how a son should act; to my grandmother Dolan, a picture of grace who taught me a little something about persistence; and to my mother, the strongest person I have ever known, whose wit, wisdom, and love have touched me more than she will ever know. And, of course, my heartfelt thanks to my father, Tom Francis Richissin, a loving and decent man who raised five sons with a firm hand and a gentle heart and who undoubtedly is in heaven right now bragging to the angels that he got his name in a book—written by one of his boys. Lord, how I miss him.

—TPR

Many thanks to my dear friend, Ken Newbaker, for his belief in me for this project; to Irene Vecchi for her not so gentle nudge to do it; to Marc Frey, for his energetic supervision; and to Frances Soo Ping Chow for her handsome book design. Special thanks to Joan Collins and Karen Pelino of Monarch Travel for always getting me an aisle; to Hassan of Duggal Labs; Bob Marion of Quaker Photo for the Kodak Photo CD scans; and Agfa's Dan Unger for the extra fifty rolls of scala film. Finally, I owe a debt of gratitude to my many coordinators: Stacy Wyn Sarno and Jon Kolbe for keeping the engine running; Michael Parker for his knowledge of California wineries; Jim Mullen for keeping Chris Elliot entertained at the Beauty Bar; Tim Mullen for helping me locate Marshall, Texas; Brian Diamond for the Alaskan connection; Bob Collins for his Alaskan hospitality and moose chili; Pilot Bob Ellis for his aerial maneuvers above the frozen tundra; Tim Cohn for his midnight Saturn Bar and cemetery tour; Bryce Lawrence for supplying Texarkana's best coconut creme pie; Tom Leonard, for his comic relief; David Barrie Gould for warming up the project; Mark Graham for his golf course navigation; Ralph Gallo of Professional Color; Florence Cupo for her comfort; and Christine Sophie Meck for her constant love and patience.

—JG

Introduction

To complete this book, it was necessary to ask the fathers and sons featured in it to speak honestly about their relationships, to present them as they are rather than as they wish them to be. All the fathers and sons you'll meet in the following pages did that. They spoke at times joyfully, at times painfully, but they all spoke frankly. And so, fair being fair, here is a bit of truth about my own father and me, a fact that is at once both joyful and painful: My relationship with my father never seemed particularly extraordinary to me, not until years after his death.

My father died when I was 31. He was a pretty good father. He coached his sons in baseball, football and basketball. He was a police officer, an honest one, a man of integrity. He put food on the table and kept enough order in a chaotic house that my four brothers and I were expected to be home to eat supper together, as a family. He was an Irish braggart about his boys, and he inflated our accomplishments to anybody who wanted to listen to him and to many people who did not. He was, as they say, a good and decent man, and I loved him and I still do.

But here is more honesty: For the longest time, I felt my father and I shared precious little with each other. I shared none of my fears with him, none of my soul. It may sound harsh, but my father and I were not friends. After little league sports, we did not do much of anything together. Our conversations were often sparse and uncomfortable, resembling those found on airplanes when two strangers are forced to sit next to each other, and for that the blame is mine. I have always worked much more diligently on my friendships than I ever did on my relationship with my father, and that is to my great regret. I never told my father I loved him; that is to my great shame. We loved each other, clearly, but we did not do a very good job of showing it.

I was well into the writing of this book before I finally took an honest look at my relationship with my father. I think I had avoided it because I feared our relationship was not extraordinary, and I did not want to acknowledge that. Writing this book, meeting the people in it, and talking to friends about it forced that honesty on me. I began to talk about my father in a way I never had—frankly and honestly—and memories that had been blocked by a misguided fear began to return.

I now recall the times as a boy that I would stand on the couch cushions, behind my sitting father, combing his hair like Dagwood Bumstead, then mussing it up and changing it to an Elvis doo. That is fun when you are a boy. My father had an imitation of Benny Hill, and when he stuck his tongue over his upper lip and batted those eyes, I would double over in hysterics. I had all but forgotten about that, but now I remember. As a little league baseball player who relied on a lack of height and a small strikezone to get on base through walks, I can recall the time I squished my eyes closed, swung the bat as hard as I could, and smacked a triple at the American Legion field. My dad was coaching me, and I remember he was the only person in Brook Park who was happier than I was. Years later, when my father would see me after I drank too much liquor, he would say, "You know, if you'd just slit your throat you'd clear up them eyes." He said it every time as if he was saying it for the first time, and it made me laugh, almost always, even when my head hurt. And when I smashed the car I had saved and saved to buy, I feared how high my father would raise his voice. He told me a smashed car was no big deal, not really, just be glad you're not hurt, boy. I know now that my father kept his voice down because he felt as bad for me as I did about the car.

Jim Graham, the photographer for this book, has had a relationship with his father that has been more complex but no less cherished. His father and mother separated before he was a toddler, and his father's visits were less than frequent. For one five-year span, Jim did not see his father at all.

Jim's father lived on the wrong side of the law, and while there's no sense glossing over his wrongdoings and his absence, there was some instinct within him that convinced Jim that his father wanted to do the right thing, even when he couldn't always pull it off. Whenever they saw each other, his father made it clear how much he loved his son, how much Jim meant to him.

It was in the sixth grade that Jim had to travel to Rahway State Prison to see his father. That's not an easy thing for a ten-year-old boy to do, but at least Jim knew where his father was. More than that, he realized that his father was beginning to turn his life around. Only a few years ago, Jim's father sat in his car and cried with his son. There were so many regrets. There always will be.

Even after prison, the long absences, and the missed opportunities, what still shines through for Jim are the times when he was a child, when his father let him sit on his lap and steer the car. And when they'd drive to the observation deck at the Philadelphia airport and watch the planes take off and land. And, especially, the time when his father told him that, yes, he was a proud father, that he liked who his son had become.

At the first dinner Jim and I had together to plot this book, we shared the stories of our fathers. It set the tone for the honesty we would seek in both words and images, trying to be careful, always, to let the relationships speak for themselves and to resist the temptation to romanticize them. Reality can stand on its own.

That reality, as you will discover in these pages, comes in many different forms. All father-son relationships have much in common—and no two are alike. The stories you'll read, are for the most part, celebratory and uplifting. But there are also moments of sadness. Honesty required that.

Both Jim and I hope this book will make you think honestly about a bond that is too often taken for granted. When Jim surveyed his relationship with his father, there were good moments to savor. When I was honest about my relationship with my father, I found in the ordinariness of it that we had a bond that was indeed extraordinary. We shared a lot, I came to realize. We were father and son.

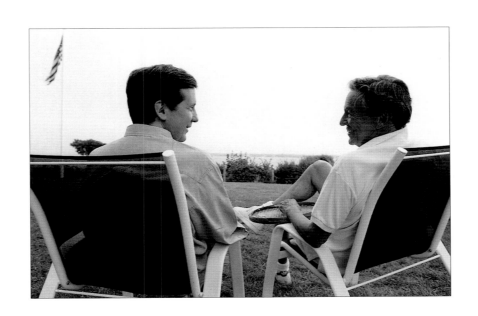

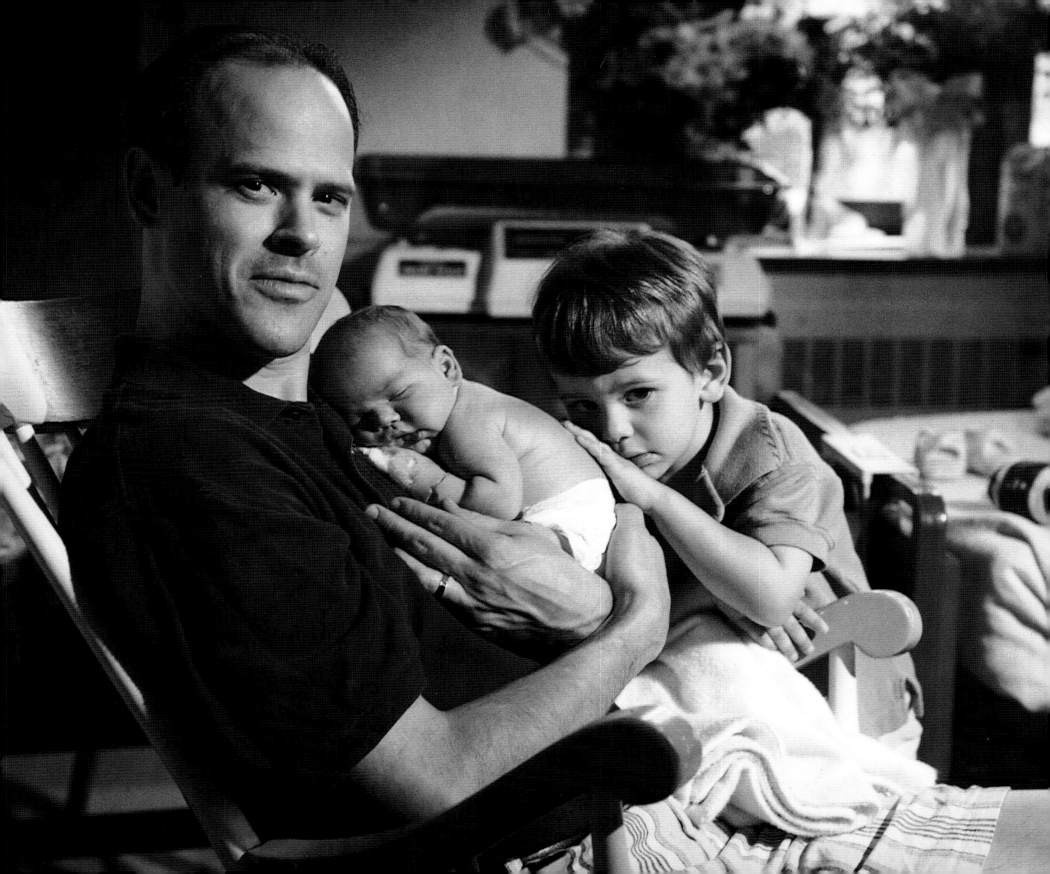

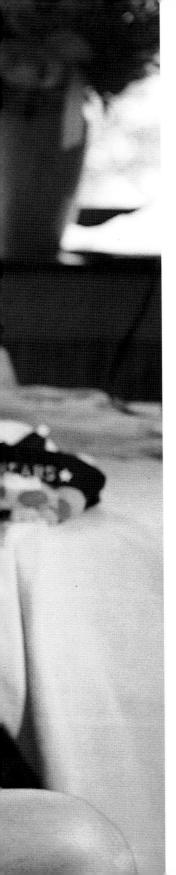

The Ryleys: Nicholas, Alexander, and William

The first baby. The first son. Worry? Concern? Wrap him in pillows with duct tape, ease him gently into the bassinet, swear not to let him out of sight until he's 25? At least?

Not for Nicholas Ryley.

"I wanted to get him out. I wanted him to see the neighborhood. I thought it was important that he hear the sounds, get the smells, feel the wind," says Ryley, in his row house in the heart of bustling South Philadelphia, sounds of the subway rattling beneath the street. So, rather than take a cab or a car home from the hospital with his new son, he bundled him up and carried him—past the hospital gardens, down antique row, by the doctor's office, a jewelry store, a city park. And home.

The first son. "We thought for sure at first that it was going to be a girl," Ryley says. "I know a lot of fathers, especially, are hoping for a boy, but I just felt like I'd be more comfortable with a little girl at first because I didn't like sports—not that it matters—and it would

Nicholas Ryley and his sons William and Alexander at Pennsylvania Hospital just after William's birth.

just somehow be a little more natural to have a little girl around."

His wife, Laureen, was checking her medical chart in the doctor's office one day, and the doctor had accidentally left evidence of the baby's gender—which the parents did not want to know. "I was looking through my chart for something else," Laureen says, "and—boom—there it was."

So much for the name Isabella.

Born in 1995, Nicholas Alexander Tavolaro Ryley—Alexander, they call him—is all about being a boy. "Remember," he interrupts his father, "that time we were out in the garden, and I had to go pee, and I peed right in the garden?" His father remembers. He remembers, too, the day his boy was born. It changed Ryley forever. That's what a firstborn son will do.

"Laureen was ready. We got a cab, told the cabbie we had to get to the hospital but that it was still a ways off and to take his time," Ryley recalls. "Well, I think he ran every stoplight on the way to the hospital. I think he'd been waiting his whole cabbie life for a moment like this." And then, twenty-two hours later, the baby was born. "I was mighty impressed. It was a great feeling. I don't think I was nervous. It was more like, I felt almost complete, like I finally did something you were supposed to do. He was a good-looking baby, with all his fingers. It was awesome.

"It's a whole new world for you," he continues. "You've continued your line, so to speak. It was pretty moving. You're worried about whether you're going to be able to be a good father and at the same time you're excited about all the possibilities."

And so new lives begin, not only for the baby, but also for his parents. When Alexander was six months old, Nicholas, who works as a salesman at a bookstore that specializes in nautical titles and charts, began taking him to work. "I think he had a great time. We set up the playpen, had some videos." That continued until the little one was about 3½. And then an event occurred that may be even more life-altering than a first son: A second son.

"It just changes the whole dynamic," Ryley explains. "To be honest, I know this sounds bad, but at first I almost resented having a second one. It was like we had our routine down and then there was this intrusion into this little life we'd built, which we all liked. It didn't take any time to get over that, though."

William Sebastian Saunders Ryley entered the world on July 7, 1998. "They let us hold him for all of about two seconds," Ryley remembers. "Then they grabbed him from us and took him away. It was like, 'jeez, did we just have a baby or what?'" William's lungs were not

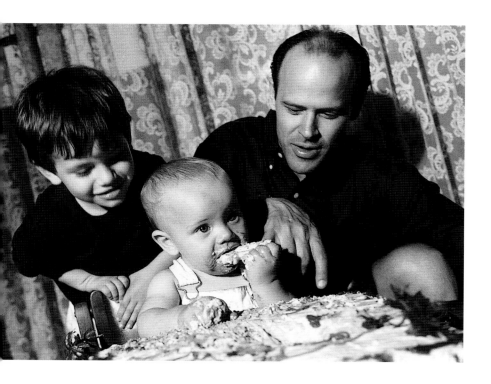

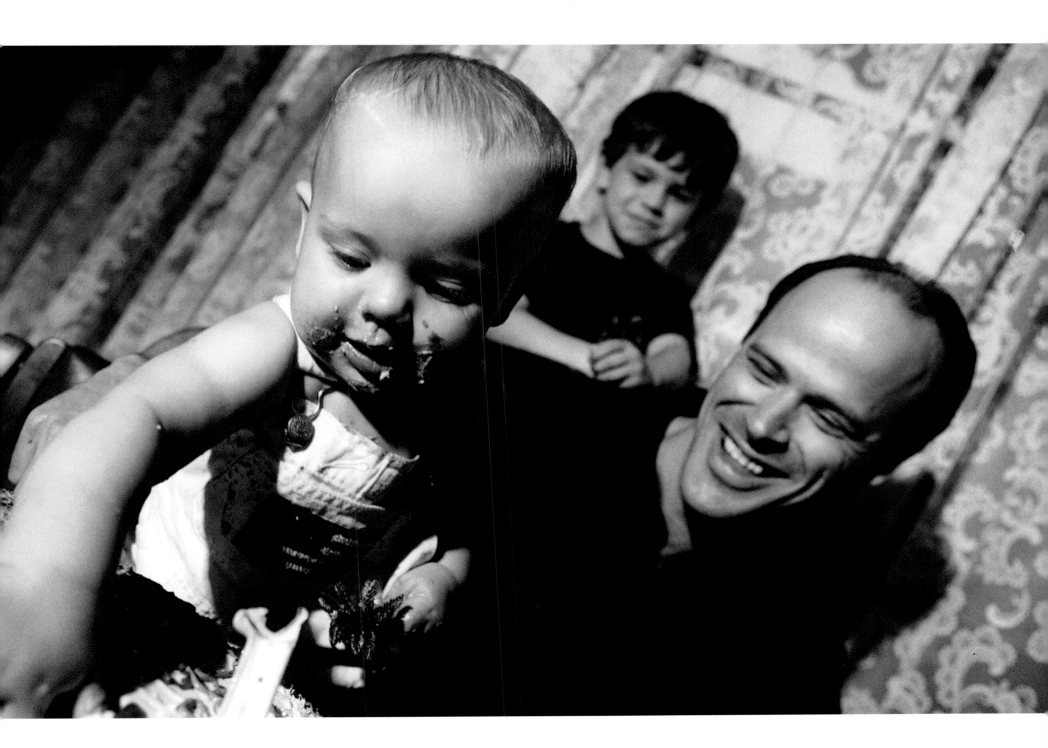

The Ryleys celebrate William's first birthday.

functioning. Doctors worked on him. He was placed in the intensive care unit for newborns. "They told us not to worry, but you do," Ryley says. "You just have to have faith that everything's going to be okay, and thankfully it was." Three days later William was released. He is healthy.

Alexander finally got to see his little brother a few days after the baby left intensive care. "In the hospital room, it was really touching," Ryley says. "Alexander had this big smile. You know, sometimes kids will act a particular way because they know they're being watched, and they know they're supposed to. This was genuine. He had this big smile and he introduced himself. He said, 'I'm your big brother Alexander, and I'm going to take care of you.'

"There were a lot of adults in the room, and a lot of them were kind of choked up."

When William was ready, Ryley carried him home as well. Just like Alexander, he wanted William to see, hear, smell, and feel the city. The baby slept the entire walk home.

When it was time for William to come to work with his father, Alexander began going to school. It was rough on him and his father. They got through it. The first son. He has been through his cowboys-and-Indians phase. He builds forts out of everything possible. He

enjoys being raucous with his little brother, stacking pillows four feet high on his head, and William—as little brothers must—is getting used to it. Alexander watches television with his parents and soaks it in. At one point, he was intrigued by a show on Zulus. "They were asking kids at school what they wanted to be when they grow up. Alexander says, 'I want to be a African!' That raised a few eyebrows," Ryley laughs, his elder son bouncing at his feet, his second son snoozing gently in his mother's arms.

For now, the father is simply enjoying his boys, watching them pass through life's early phases. Alexander began walking just as he turned one year old. For Ryley, the feeling of seeing a second son take his first steps was just as powerful.

"It's a pretty big milestone," he says of William's wobbling forward. "He was pleased as punch. You could really tell by looking at him that he'd entered a whole new world. He's more animated now. He has even more of a personality."

"With one, it was kind of like a novelty, something we really just loved," Ryley says. "With two, it's a bit more like a job. But I can say, in all honesty, it's the greatest thing in the world, certainly the greatest thing that's ever happened to me."

The Lockes: Jimmy, Gary, and Dylan

Washington Governor Gary Locke, his father Jimmy, and son Dylan in the governor's mansion.

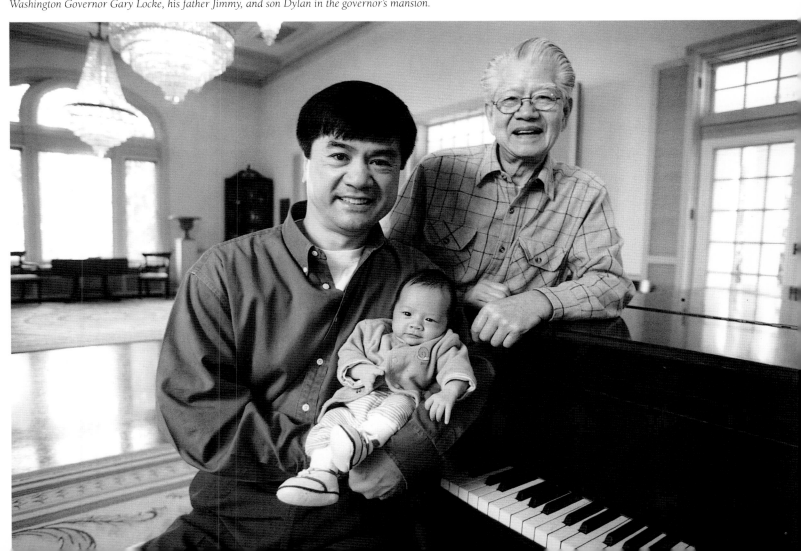

The people of the tiny farming hamlet of Jilong could forget, at least for one day, about the squalor surrounding them. The village, in China's Guangdong Province, has no toilets, no running water, houses without roofs. But on this day the villagers were lined up to celebrate.

They were gathered to cheer an American success story: One of their own was returning to the land where his father grew up, returning as the first Chinese-American governor in the United States. Banners flying overhead welcomed "the return of Gov. Gary Locke to Home Town."

"I was starting to cry I was so overwhelmed by the people who turned out," the Washington governor recalls from his office in Olympia's marble-stacked capitol. "I remember seeing the room where my father was born. It had no electricity and an open roof where rainwater would come in. I felt like I was stepping back in time . . . it was such a long trip but it was invigorating when we got there."

If the trip to the village was long—the marathon flight was followed by a four-hour hydrofoil ride from Hong Kong—it was nothing compared to Locke's journey to the highest office in Washington. Spanning generations, the family's story is the familiar one of immigrants coming to the United States, but the hardships that they overcame and the success that they realized is the stuff of movies.

At the turn of the century, the grandfather, Gim, came to the United States and worked as a houseboy not a mile from the capitol where Gary Locke now serves. Returning to China, he married, raised a son to his teens, and then brought his children—including the governor's father, Jimmy—to Seattle. Having escaped the poverty of their homeland, the Lockes soon were faced with America's Great Depression. To survive, the grandfather and Jimmy worked in a Seattle hospital, returning home with scraps of food from the hospital kitchen to feed the family.

Jimmy Locke survived the Depression to raise his own family.

Although he participated in the invasion of Normandy—coming ashore just after D-day—as a member of the U.S. Army, he was forced to endure the slurs and indignities that his generation of Asian immigrants faced. Undeterred, he worked fourteen-hour days at a restaurant and grocery store to pull his wife and children out of public housing and, as it turned out, help usher his son into the governor's mansion.

"I worked seven days a week," says Jimmy Locke, now in his eighties. "As a parent, you always want to work hard, put your kids through college so they don't have to go through what we did. I tell my kids, you study hard, and you go to college, and then you get a good job."

Not even Jimmy Locke, though, thought his son Gary would become so wildly successful, certainly not in politics. When Gary Locke announced he wanted to go into politics, the father was against it. "He was a good, intelligent boy," the father recalls. "He was good in math,

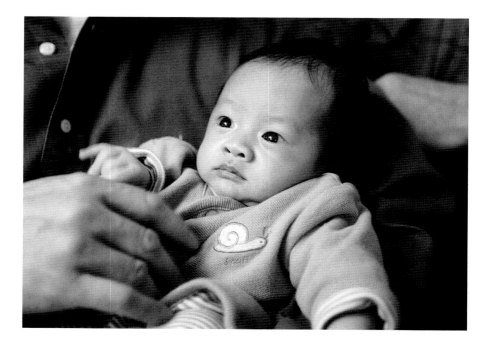

good in physics. He could have been a scientist, like a chemist or something, but here he goes into politics. I say, 'Politics pays no money and it's only headaches.' He say, 'Everything else is too dull.' So politics it was."

In 1982, having graduated from Yale University and Boston University Law School, Gary Locke returned to Washington and decided to run for a state House seat. Running against a popular incumbent in a crowded primary field, conventional wisdom said he didn't stand a chance.

"I told him, 'Gee, you're going to have a tough time'," Jimmy Locke recalls. "He said, 'Well, you have to try.' I said, 'Okay, then make a go of it. I'll help you.'"

Retired by this time, the father went door to door canvassing for his son, then spent hours more crafting political signs touting the Locke name, then hours more on whatever else he could do.

In the general election, Gary Locke won his seat with 82 percent of the vote.

"Dad was tremendously supportive," the governor recalls. "He built these signs with nails and glue and staples. He made food for the campaign workers. He did whatever he could do."

Locke served eleven years in the Washington State Legislature, rising to chairman of the House Appropriations Committee, where he wielded enormous power fashioning the state's budgets. In 1992, he again had news for his father: He was contemplating a run for governor.

"People wanted him to run," Jimmy recalls. "I said, 'No, don't run yet. Your name is not well enough known—and besides, you're single. The governor has a mansion, so you have to have a first lady.'"

Gary Locke's first marriage had ended in divorce, and he had been single for years. His father's good advice notwithstanding, it was another Democrat's entry into the race that convinced him to bypass the 1992 election. In the meantime, he spent three years as King County

Executive, and married a television newscaster, Mona Lee. In 1996, with his father's support, he ran for governor and won.

"Back in China, when you get to that position, it's like a dream, especially in our village," Jimmy says. "Nobody ever had that kind of a position in America—not even a high position in China, not from our village."

The Lockes' journey, though, did not end when Gary Locke moved into the governor's mansion. The journey of a struggling family from a poor province in China was not quite complete. That would not come until last year, when the governor had a son of his own, Dylan, about two years after daughter Emily. Now, the most recent Locke is not referred to as "the son of Chinese immigrants," but as "the governor's son."

"For me, the transition became complete with Dylan's arrival," the governor says. "Now I'm following in the steps of my grandfather and my father. What they did was motivated by attention to children. The purpose in life was to raise a family. I'm just really so thankful for the love and unconditional support my parents gave me. If I can make those same sacrifices and be as nurturing and emotionally supportive to Dylan and Emily, I'll be happy."

Because of the governor's success, Dylan is not likely to face some of the same challenges his great-grandfather, grandfather, and father faced. He most likely, in fact, has entered the world with a leg up.

Gary Locke plans, someday, to take another trip to China. He wants to go unannounced next time, no reporters jostling him, watching his every move, no people from the village lining the rice paddies and the narrow streets to herald him.

"I'd like to go sometime with Dylan and Emily, hopefully with Dad, and really get a chance to soak it all in this time," the governor says. "I'd like to show it to them and let them know, this is where you came from."

The McEnroes: John P., John, Mark, and Patrick

"We weren't raising professional athletes," insists John P. McEnroe, who, in fact, raised precisely that with his wife, Katherine, whether they meant to or not. "That was nothing that we had in mind when we were raising our kids. We were just raising kids, hoping they would become good, well-educated citizens." Later he asks one of the many journalists approaching him with questions about his sons, "This isn't going to be all about tennis, is it? I don't want it to be all about tennis."

Make no mistake: John P. McEnroe is a father grateful for the success his sons have had on the tennis court. He bursts with pride over the accomplishments of eldest son John, the three-time Wimbledon, four-time U.S. Open champion. At age 21, John became the youngest-ever number 1 player in the world, a rank he held at four consecutive year ends. He knows that third son, Patrick, while not enjoying John's level of success—few tennis players in history have—has had a tennis career that many would envy, including more

From left, Patrick, Mark, John P., and John McEnroe before a tournament in New York.

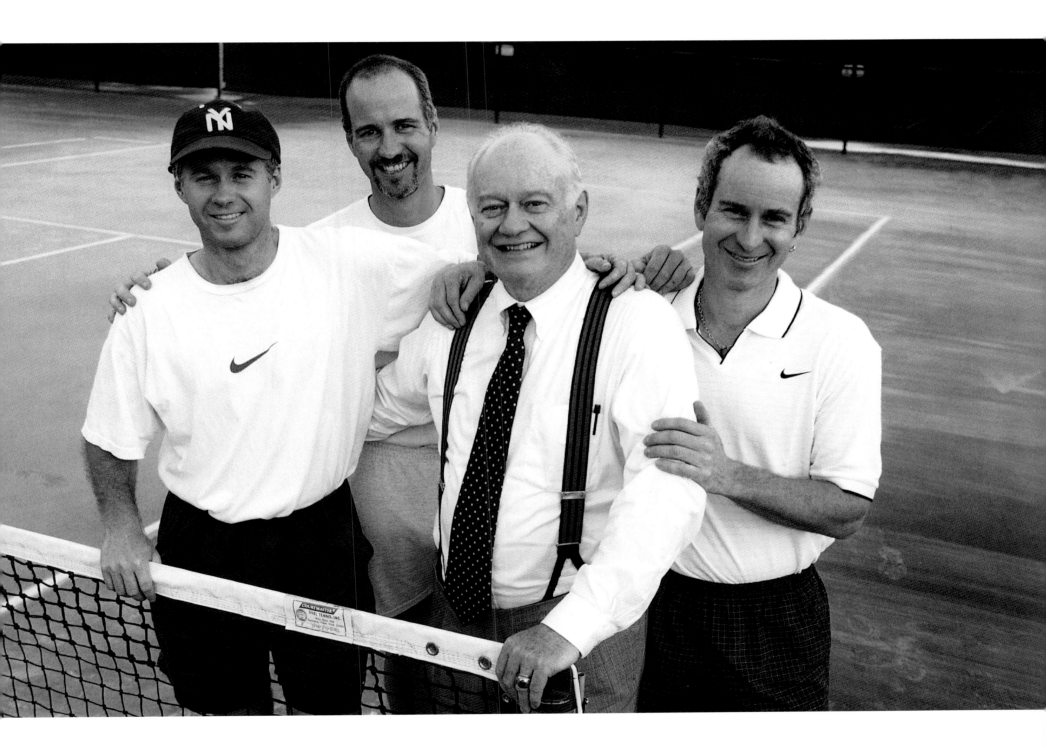

than a dozen titles. And his middle son, Mark, who chose law over tennis, was a high school All-American, a member of the University of Stanford team, and yearly plays with John in a doubles tournament on the senior tour, although without success to date. "I've disproved the theory that John and anybody is the best doubles team in tennis," jokes Mark.

The father was a familiar fixture in the stands when all of his sons were playing—still is at age 64—visible to millions of tennis fans when John and Patrick were collecting tennis titles around the world, and he regularly refers to their professional careers as "smashing."

But while tennis has tended to define the family publicly over the past two decades (even as John McEnroe has been one of the defining forces in the game), there is more to this group of scrappy battlers than a lot of racquet. They are a clan full of Irish wit and self-deprecation and barbs for each other that are always aimed at the funnybone and not the heart. ("I remember once acting like a total ass—" John begins one story. "—I take exception to that," his father interrupts. "I wouldn't say a *total* ass." When Mark isn't smiling enough for a family photo before a doubles tournament with John, his brother explains: "You have to understand. He's lucky to be standing. He's about to throw up.") More importantly for the father, there are stories of triumphs against great odds that had nothing to do with tennis, and with the McEnroe brothers there is a genuine admiration for the patriarch of the family and a bond between father, sons, and brothers that is as true as a hard-court bounce.

"I want people to know how close this family is," says the father, who is known as John P. "I want people to know how my sons love each other, and on occasion they even love their parents. Not everything is tennis."

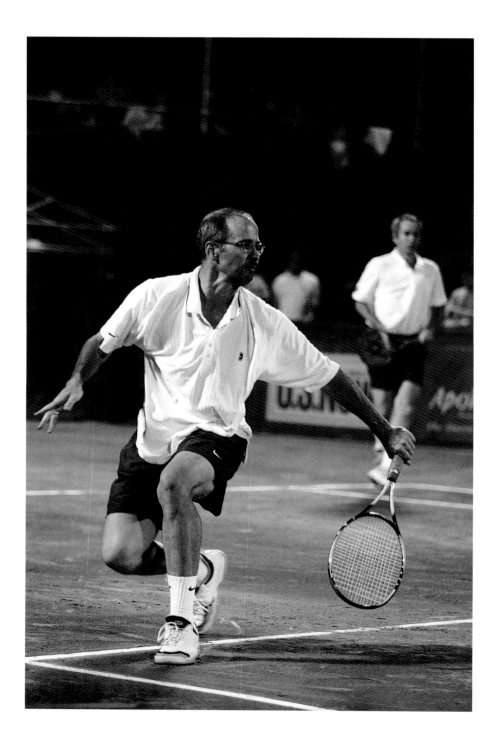

Certainly not. But there is a little-remarked upon irony to the intense scrutiny that American sports icons are subjected to. That is, despite all the attention they receive from the media, they are often the subjects of lazy, shorthand journalism, which tends to label and classify. In this manner the McEnroes have for years been reduced to a story line, one that fails to provide insight into who they are and why they are. John's successes have been so impressive—and his personality so strong—that the shorthand has spilled over to the family. He is brash on the court (and now while announcing televised matches), it is often written, because of the drive he witnessed in his father, who grew up in a fourth-floor Manhattan walkup, the son of working-class Irish immigrants, to become a wealthy, high-powered New York attorney.

"But it's definitely not that simple," John says. "Dad had a lot of drive and still does. But don't underestimate my mother. She's pretty strong. When I think about it, the nicer part of me is probably from my dad. The rougher part—and I say this with love—probably comes from my mother."

An example? John P. recalls: "I remember coming home and I got my grades from law school. I was second in the class, and I tell my wife, 'Isn't this wonderful? Second in the class!' She said, 'See, had you worked harder you could have been first.' By the way, the next year I was first."

But the fact is John P. *was* driven. He worked full-time during the day, attended Fordham Law School at night, all while supporting John and Mark, who had already arrived. After graduating, he lived the life of the young attorney trying to make partner, putting in twelve- to fifteen-hour days with the firm of Paul, Weiss, Rifkind, Wharton & Garrison.

"I really don't know that his drive relates to our tennis all that much," agrees Patrick. "He didn't even pick up the game until his early thirties.

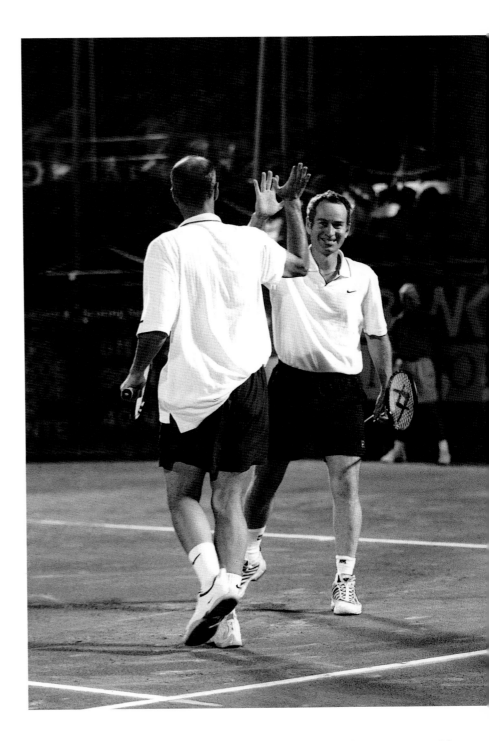

He'd try to coach us, but his strategy was something like, 'Go out there and win the first game, then go out and win the third game.' At the same time, when I think I have it tough, I think of him working his way up from nothing. He was driven to succeed, certainly. I remember him saying, 'If you're going to go out there, give 100 percent—or don't do it.'"

John P. gave it 100 percent, plus. He drove his kids to tennis matches on the weekends, never complaining. And he pushed on at the law firm. When John turned 15, his father called him at the tennis academy John was attending. John P. had made partner.

"That's probably the proudest I've ever been for him," John recalls. "This was a monumental thing for him. It was like winning Wimbledon would be for me. It was a moment when I just knew it was something. . . . It gave me the chills."

Mark followed in his father's footsteps, not pursuing a tennis career and instead becoming an attorney. He thinks John P.'s drive has been passed down to John, especially, but it's not the blind ambition that has been portrayed. Proof is in that seniors tournament Mark and John annually play together.

"John and Patrick played together a few times for real," Mark says. "This is John doing something nice for me, and he gets a kick out of it. It's kind of surreal to have a brother be the best at anything, and I guess my father's drive has been passed most to him, but so has the compassionate side."

John McEnroe is now married to the rock singer/songwriter Patty Smyth and he has become something of a musician himself, performing occasionally with a group called The Johnny Smyth Band. He has six kids; Mark has three. Patrick recently got married and an episode at his bachelor party may provide a genuine glimpse of what the family is about. The brothers were jamming and, as usual, they wanted to get

their father in on the act. Call it a generation gap or call it good sense, but John P. never took the time to learn the lyrics to "Sympathy for the Devil" by the Rolling Stones.

The sons were undeterred. They went to their father and explained how it was to be done. And the father, obliging, stepped into the jam. His job was easy enough, and the performance brought down the house.

"We said, just say 'Hoo-Hoo' when we do, and he did," Mark says. "He said it was one of the highlights of his life."

These days, John is trying to get his father to spend more time with the grandchildren—and John P. is taking some extra time with them, though he shows no signs of slowing. "I'm trying to get him into the grandpa thing," John explains. "With me not being on the road so much now, he gets to see them more." And, all of the sons have fond memories of their father watching them hit the ball around—he was laughing at them, not barking instructions.

"He has an undying pride in his family and his boys," Patrick says. "There was nothing he liked more than sitting out on the porch and watching his boys on the tennis court, and you're thinking, *God, Dad, can't you do something else*? Now, we look back on it and it's kind of heartwarming."

John P. recalls those days. But he stresses, yet again, that sports are just part of the family—that the family isn't all about sports, and certainly not all about winning.

"Here's what I will say," says John P. "We weren't raising professional athletes but at the same time, we taught them winning is better than losing, it's better to finish first than second. I think we've all got a competitive streak in us, but if you're going to be successful at anything, you have to want it."

The Aycocks: Charlie, Al, and Alan

From left, Al, Alan, and Charlie Aycock stand guard at North Carolina's Fort Bragg.

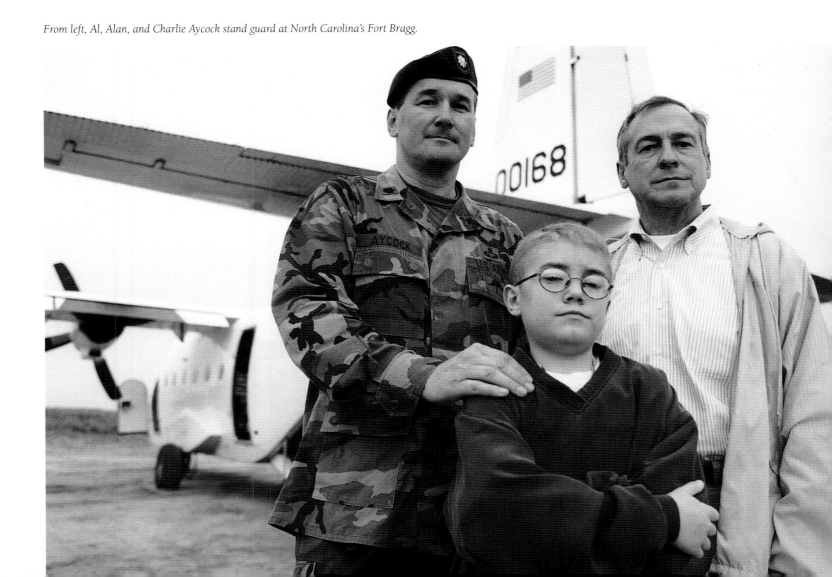

When word reached Charlie Aycock that his grandson was slipping away, that almost a year after enduring a double-lung transplant the boy's kidneys had failed, he found himself in the middle of a family meeting. To his side sat his sons, Al, the boy's father, and Steven, the boy's uncle.

Before Al or his brother could speak, Charlie, the patriarch of the family, raised his hand. "We're going to need a transplant," he said, not holding much hope that the boy's kidneys would recover. "Now, we know we're all going to be matches, but there's nothing either of you have to do with this. I'm right here. It's mine he's getting. End of discussion."

At 13, Alan Aycock Jr. did indeed need a transplant, and after more than a year of dialysis treatments he got one. As he lay on a gurney in pre-op at Duke University Medical Center, he looked and saw his grandfather, also on a gurney. Charlie Aycock was there to give his grandson one of his kidneys, just as he said he would. When the hospital technicians arrived to roll the grandfather to the operating room, he and his only grandson looked at each other. Young Alan raised a thumbs-up. His grandfather did the same.

"Watching that, my father and my son going into surgery at the same time, it was overwhelming," says Al. "I was touched beyond words. It's something I'll never forget."

For Charlie, a retired lieutenant colonel, coming to the aid of his grandson—and the son who gave him a grandchild—was as natural as a salute. He had, after all, served in the Vietnam War as a Green Beret, running a platoon that conducted long-range reconnaissance and harassment of the Ho Chi Minh trail network. Then, when he was promoted from first lieutenant to captain, he worked in the counter-terrorist and anti-Viet Cong infrastructure unit.

"I never had to think twice," Charlie says of his decision, Alan to his side, healthy more than a year after the operation. "It just seemed to be the thing to do." There is no hint of false machismo in his tone. In fact, his voice begins to falter and his eyes begin to tear when he talks about it, so he makes a joke to bring his emotions under control. "I told him, this kidney is already broken in, so you'll probably be getting up in the middle of the night to go to the bathroom. Be ready."

The Aycocks are a family that has always been willing to sacrifice for others. Including his service in Vietnam, Charlie was on active duty for thirteen years, served seven more years as a reservist, and now, as a civilian, works as chief of operations for the army's Special Forces Command. His job entails running logistics for deployments from Fort Bragg, North Carolina, sending Special Operations Forces worldwide in support of Commanders-in-Chief and U.S. ambassadors. On the day he retired from the army, he passed his Green Beret to his son Al—who graduated that very day from Special Forces School. Currently a lieutenant colonel, Al has also built an impressive career in the army. He has been sent around the world in the name of peace, to Egypt immediately after the assassination of Anwar Sadat, to Tunisia on an exercise following the Palestinian Liberation Organization's move there. During Desert Shield and Desert Storm, he served on the Crisis Action Team and has been a Special Operations Action Officer for a program that is still classified. Most recently, Al served as assistant chief of staff at Fort Bragg, working in the same building as his father. He's now at the Army War College in Carlisle Barracks, Pennsylvania, the same college from which his father graduated. When he graduates, he likely will soon become a general.

"There are a lot of similarities," says Charlie, now 61. "Of course, I wanted him to go into Special Forces, but I never tried to push him into anything. I just tried to set a good example for him." He continues: "You know, with Al going through Special Forces School, he always had to put up with, 'Oh, Aycock? Are you Charlie's boy? Must be Charlie Aycock's boy.' Now he's a good father and has built his own career in Special Forces Command, and now I'm happy to be known as Al Aycock's dad."

Charlie and Al's close relationship is all the more remarkable because duty called Charlie away during much of Al's childhood. And, because Al's mother and Charlie's wife, Rebecca Ann, died when Al was 4 years old, he lived mostly with his grandmother. "I didn't grow up with my father, but he's the one who mentored me and told me what I needed to do without telling me what to do," Al says. "That's a tough thing for a father to do."

Despite the frequent absences, Al and Charlie forged a relationship that few fathers and sons have shared. When Al graduated from the U.S. Military Academy, for example, it was his father who administered the officer's oath. On graduation day from Special Forces School, Charlie and Al jumped from a plane together and Charlie pinned the Parachutist's Badge on his son. Finally, their relationship culminated in Charlie giving part of himself, literally, to Alan, so that Alan could live. Charlie's act also allowed Al to continue his career, which involves no small number of jumps from airplanes.

It's a tough job, but not quite as tough, as not knowing whether your son will make it another year, another day, another hour. At one point, recalls Al's wife, Sue, the doctors told them, "You might just want to make him comfortable and let him go." They weren't sure whether he'd last another minute.

Letting him go wasn't an option. Alan's problems were discovered shortly after birth. His faulty lungs were treated, but they wouldn't last him into his late teens. When the donor lungs became available, he hopped into a helicopter and was flown to Duke Medical Center while his parents sped down Interstate 40 for the hour-plus drive to the hospital.

The operation was a success. But a year and two days later, Alan's kidneys shut down. After six months in the hospital and more than a year as an outpatient on dialysis, doctors successfully performed the kidney transplant. For reasons his doctors have never quite understood, however, Alan took a turn for the worse just days after the operation. He had the flu, but that didn't explain the severity of his condition.

"I can remember him in the hospital, the closest we came to losing him," recalls his mother. "He couldn't breathe, and he was waving good-bye, and he told me to tell his father that we had been good parents."

Alan, of course, survived. When doctors x-rayed his transplanted kidney, they saw that a barrier of some kind of fluid—still unknown—had formed around it. "It was like his body knew, okay, this is the flu, we have to protect his new kidney," Sue says. Adds Al, "We joke that all those years my father had in the Special Forces trained his kidney to recognize the enemy."

Alan is forever grateful to the anonymous family who donated their young daughter's lungs. But knowing that his grandfather's kidney is keeping him alive is especially meaningful. "I don't know the family that gave me the lungs, but I know they're good people," Alan says. "But I know my grandfather, so of course it's special. It's unbelievable, really."

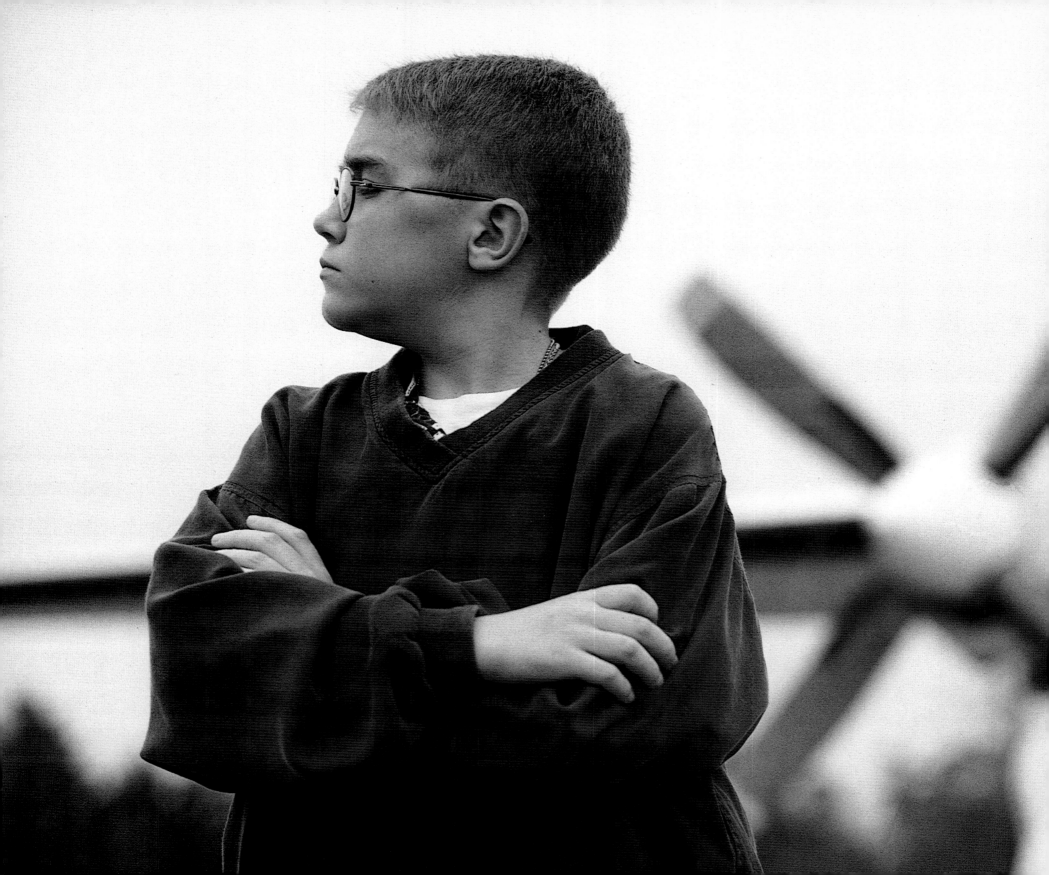

Now 16, the medical problems and months and months in hospitals have left Alan looking younger than his age, but doctors are confident he'll hit a growth spurt. He golfs ("I hit a 42—put *that* in the book," he says), skis, and recently he took a whitewater rafting trip with his church group. Not bad for a guy who less than a year earlier was in a hospital bed fighting for his life.

Through it all, the family pulled together, relying heavily on its Baptist roots and friends and family, including Alan's adopted sister, Jennifer, and Charlie's second wife, Anne. And Charlie, ever the good soldier, went through the operation and recovery without a complaint. He was working full time a month after the operation that removed his kidney.

Although traumatic, the experience not only saved Alan's life, but also worked to bring the family together emotionally: Al provided Charlie a grandson; by donating his kidneys, Charlie allowed Al to keep his son.

"There's just a bond between fathers and sons and grandsons that is indescribable in its power, especially when there is mutual respect and love and understanding between everyone involved," Al says. "What happened with Alan, that caused us to grow even closer than I could have ever imagined."

Alan looks at his father and his grandfather. He has never been closer to them, rarely has had a future that looked so bright. He knows what they have done for their country and he knows what they have done for him. Succinctly, as is his manner, he sums up.

"I think," he says, "this family is a miracle."

The Bartletts: Bo, Will, Man, and Eliot

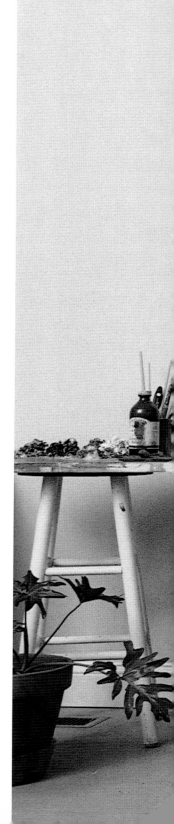

One rule in the Bartlett house is simple but absolute: When the kids turn 18, they are no longer kids. They are adults. And so they are on their own, no more living in the family home just outside Philadelphia.

Although it may sound harsh, Bo Bartlett, the father, did not institute the rule with his wife, Melanie, out of anything but love. He does not insist that his three sons do anything in particular. He does insist that whatever they do, they do it well. An artist himself, he will, without hesitation, encourage them through his own example to take a chance on the arts, to realize that it is possible to succeed as painters, musicians, writers—whatever they want to be. But if they have not found their direction by age 18, he will push them out the door to find their way.

"It's not an attitude of 'you can't live here,'" Bartlett explains. "It's about, at 18, you have to start making some choices about what your life is going to look like. Instead of being children at home, they need to get their lives going."

From left, Eliot, Will, Bo, and Man Bartlett pose in Bo's home studio.

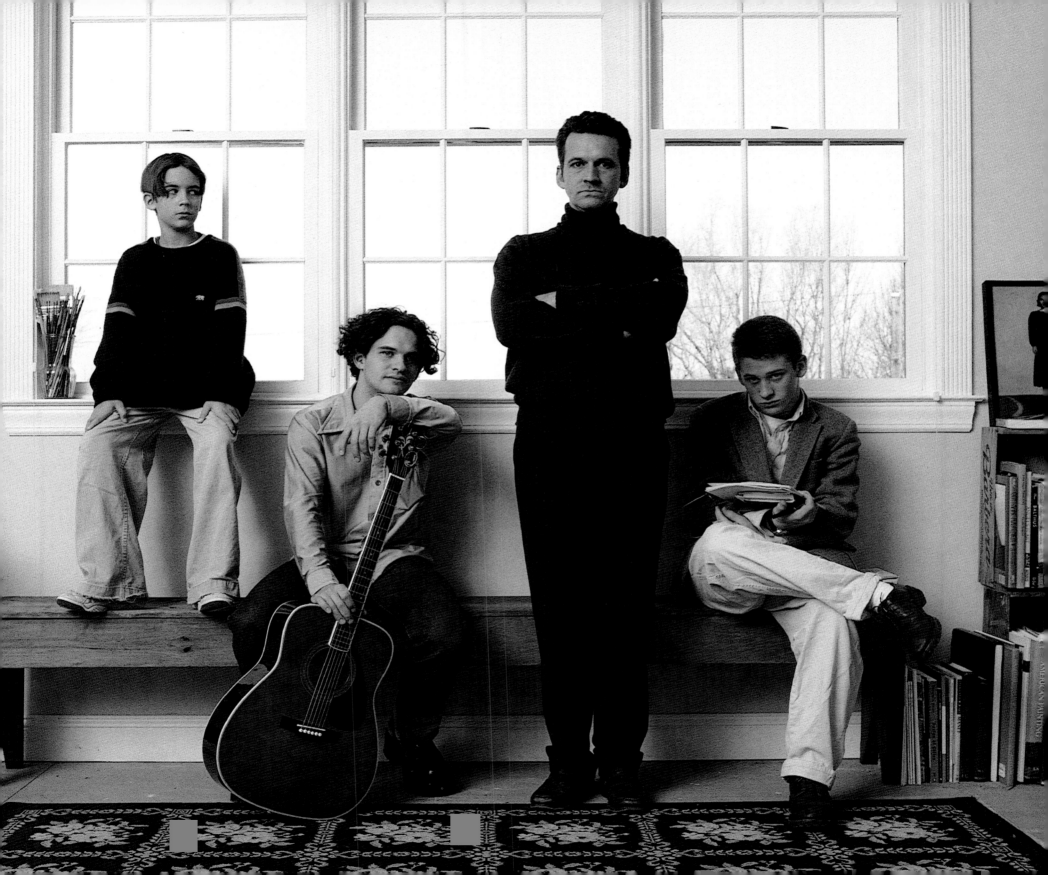

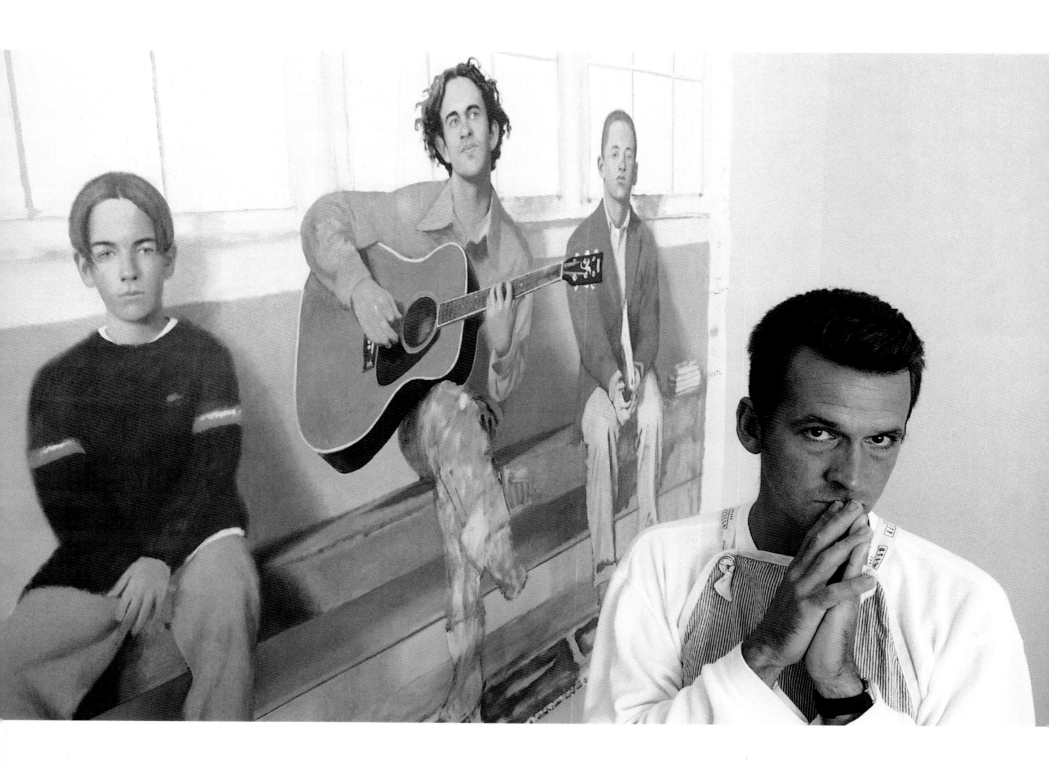

His sons, all three of them, are listening. William, 23, is the wild-haired musician, inventing his own brand of music, a techno-influenced "folk electronica." Man (short for Emmanuel), 18, is the dreamer, the poet, the neatly trimmed, spectacled screenwriter-in-waiting. Eliot, all of 11 years old, may prove to be the truest artist, painting or drawing his way through life, just like his father, who has made a very successful career as an oil painter. (The artist Andrew Wyeth had this to say about Bo Bartlett: "I'm a pretty critical old man. There are very few young American artists whose work I find exciting. One of them happens to be my son, Jamie. The other is Bo Bartlett. They've got it. It's there. Keep a close watch on their future.") It will be some time before it's clear whether the sons can live well off the arts in a financial sense, but already the father is encouraged that they appear willing to give it a go. It hasn't been easy with all of them.

"I've tried to live a creative life and show them that it can be rewarding on many levels," says Bo. "They'll learn if they can do it or not. I tell them it takes perseverance. There are all kinds of degrees of talent out there, but sometimes it's not the people with all the talent who make it. Sometimes it's the people with the chutzpah." It was with talent as well as "chutzpah" that Bo Bartlett has achieved critical and financial success as an artist. And his success did not come without some help from the very sons he is now encouraging: He uses them as models in many of his paintings, at times whimsical, at other times almost disturbing.

Bo Bartlett is not preaching the arts or finding direction in life to his sons without ever having taken a chance himself. His father worked in the family business, designing furniture and the interiors of department stores. He was successful, and Bartlett could have followed in his footsteps, but he did not consider it an option. At 18 years old, he packed a trunk and went to Florence, Italy.

"I thought I'd be a European artist for a long time. Then she sent me a letter," he says with a nod to wife Melanie. "She said she was pregnant. I sent a letter back saying, 'Good.'" After six months in Florence, Bartlett returned to the United States and William was born. "We didn't make choices," the father says. "Our choices made us."

All of Barlett's sons' lives are still taking shape. For Will, it has been a struggle to pull his life together—though he is the first to admit the 18-and-out rule helped.

"When you're out on your own, just kind of moving around and pretty broke, you start to think about what you want to do with your life. I can't say that made it any easier, but it certainly made it more necessary and definitely more immediate."

Now living in New York's Gramercy Park, he's putting on shows with his techno-music, but for years he bounced around the country, more or less aimlessly, trying, as he describes it, "to find my soul. That was my little line—I'm out finding my soul."

Unlike with his younger brothers, his father's renown as an artist worked against him for some time. "Since my dad has been successful most of my life, I have issues with success," Will says. "It's like, how do you live up to someone who's always been successful? Growing up and figuring out how I was supposed to be as successful in my art as he is in his, that's been difficult. The truth is, I have basically no faith in myself. The faith comes from everyone else, including my dad, so that's been as much of his influence on me than anything."

For Man, though, Bo's success has had just the opposite effect. "The fact that he's a painter is a huge boost to me," Man says. "The fact that he makes a living doing it is really motivational. To have someone close to me who does what he loves to do is really inspiring. It says, 'Yeah, you can do what you want.'"

He plans to attend college to pursue theater or some form of writing. Attending college satisfies the "18 rule" at the Bartlett house, and the kids will always be welcome back home on breaks. College, declare Bo and Melanie, is a direction.

"It says a person has an idea of what he wants his life to be, and that's all that rule is about," says Melanie. "There were some painful times with Will, but it was something that had to be done."

For Eliot, who at a young age has shown the most promise as a painter, the father has not provided only inspiration, but technical advice. Every Saturday morning at 10 o'clock, he gets an art lesson. ("He could do shadow and light," boasts the father, "when he was 5 years old. 5!") Eliot would be happy to go the artist route, whether it be musician, a lighting designer, an actor, or a painter.

"I don't really think being a lawyer would be good," he says. "I don't want to fight over stuff. I think being an artist would be good. It's all inspiration from my dad, I guess. He tells me to keep on trying, don't get discouraged. When it's rainy and I'm bored, he tells me to go draw."

The father, though, won't tell them all to be artists, not if they don't want to be. Art, after all, is supposed to come from within. So he will sit by, not silently but quietly, nudging his sons, not pushing them.

"Sure, I'd love for them all to be in the arts," Bartlett says. "How could I not? But I want them to follow what they want to follow. The thing that makes them feel most wholly alive is the thing they ought to follow. We try to live by that philosophy of going with your deepest instincts of what you should do. I don't know what that is for the boys. I can't make decisions for them, but I can try to guide them."

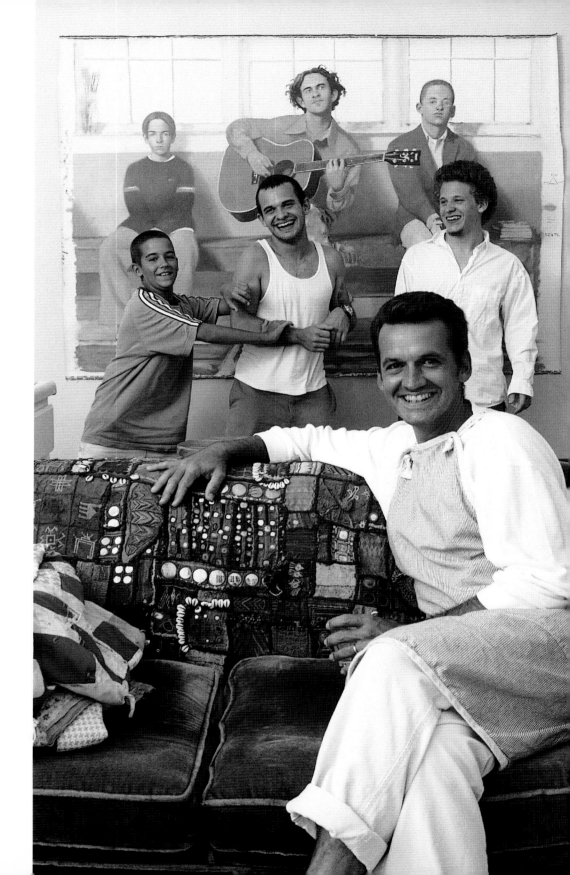

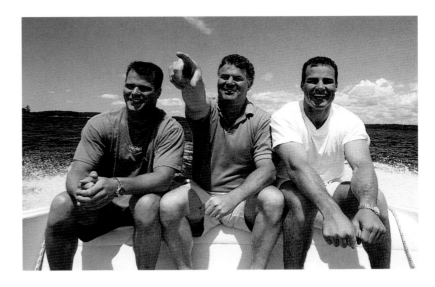

The Lindroses: Carl, Eric, and Brett

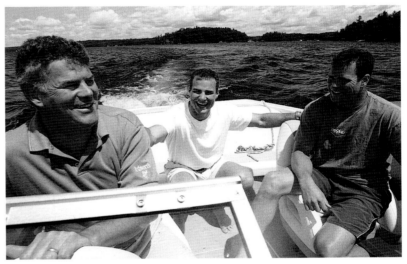

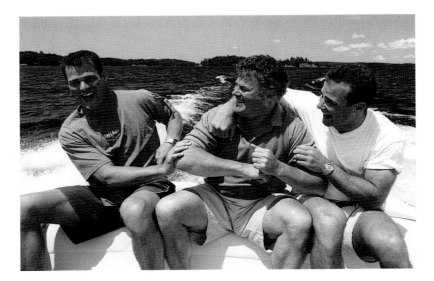

Bottom photo: From left, Brett, Carl, and Eric Lindros go for a spin on Lake Rosseau.

It could have been so easy for Eric Lindros and his family. He could have kept his mouth shut and smoothly glided through life like he now does on the ice as one of the National Hockey League's premier players. His father, Carl, his top advisor—who would become his agent—could have recommended that Eric negotiate with the team that drafted him, the Nordiques, and both would have been assured delirious cheers from rabid hockey fans in Quebec.

There was only one problem with all that: Eric Lindros and his father didn't want to do what they thought was easy. They wanted to do what they thought was right.

The Lindroses are a close family who have always stuck together over principle. And two principles in particular tend to define them: They will base their decisions on what's best for the family member involved; and however hard the knocks get—and however much money they make—the business side of hockey will not alter their personal lives, which are centered on each other. That they have managed to accomplish the latter is all the more impressive when you consider their hockey lives and personal lives are so tightly intertwined, with Carl both father and business agent to Eric and, not long ago, to younger son Brett, who also played in the NHL but took his doctors' advice and chose to preserve his health rather than seek further glory.

But Carl has always been a father first, one not immune to barbs from his sons. When Carl was in school, he was president of the art club, Eric feels compelled to mention. "People would say, 'Oh, what dramatic pictures—those wild colors! Fabulous!'" he says, exaggerating the reaction to his father's work. "Well, what they didn't know was he was color blind."

"That didn't deter me," his father reminds him.

"Yeah, he went to clay," Eric says.

While Eric's ribbing was lighthearted, that same type of determination was evident when the family—including Eric and Brett's mother Bonnie—took on two entrenched hockey establishments. When Eric was drafted in 1989 by the Canadian junior-hockey system's Sault Ste. Marie Greyhounds, his father and mother helped him gather as much information on his options as they could, then Eric decided Sault Ste. Marie was not the place to play. It was nearly 400 miles away, few of them by four-lane highway, about a nine-hour drive across Ontario from the Lindros's Toronto home, and Eric was 16. He knew he couldn't graduate from high school in a timely fashion given the amount of travel that playing for Sault Ste. Marie would require.

"The reason was pretty straight-forward from our end," Eric recalls. "We thought what we were doing was right. When the team's own educational advisor sits in your living room and says you can't accommodate the educational load, you can't go. You never know when you'll fall to injury, and you have to have a backup plan, and school is it."

"What we wanted, and thought we could handle," Carl adds, "was a three-hour drive. We had three children and we couldn't devote all of our time to Eric."

Surely, people would understand the family's reasoning. This was a kid. But people didn't understand, not a lot of them anyway. Hockey is close to a national religion in Canada, and Eric's refusal to play there was seen by some as blasphemous. As much furor as his decision raised, it was as if ice north of the United States had been willed to the Devil. While some people sided with the Lindroses, others were vicious in their verbal attacks, including some

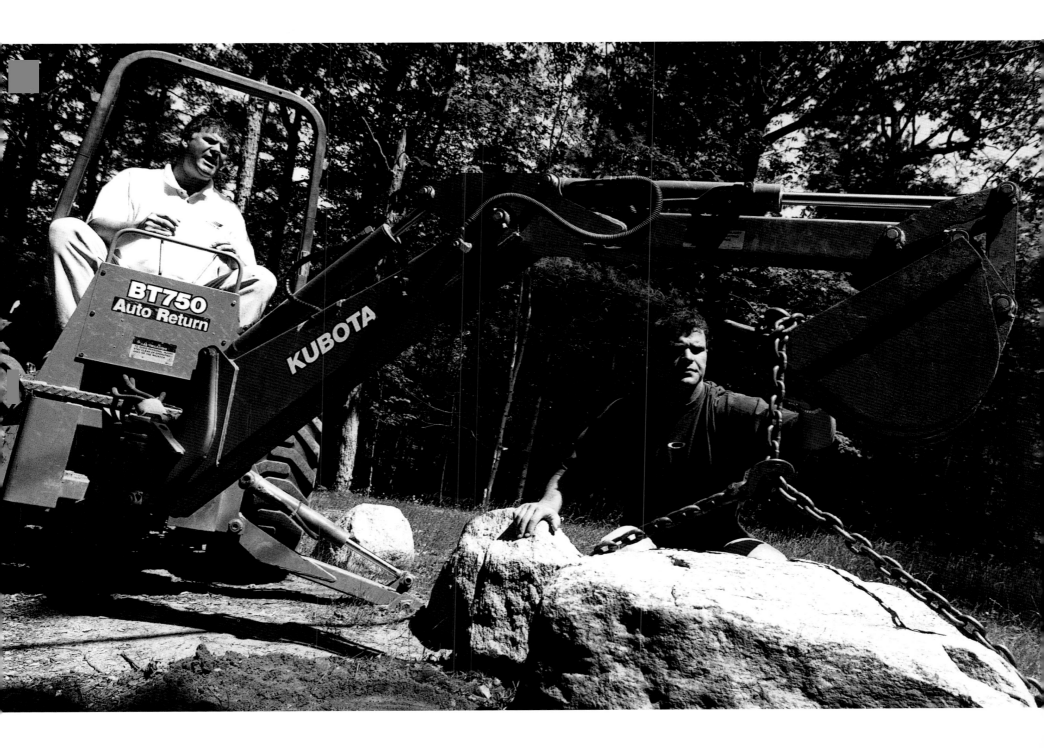

against his mother. They didn't see a close-knit family fighting for principle but a spoiled kid and doting parents who demanded their way or no way.

The Lindroses, undeterred, stuck to their guns; Eric enrolled in high school in Farmington, Michigan—less than three hours away—and played in an American junior league. Already known throughout Canada as the country's top NHL prospect, Eric was suddenly lost to the Ontario Hockey League, intending to enroll at the University of Michigan the next year. Realizing it had let its top draw slide away, the league changed its bylaws so a team could trade its first-round pick. Eric was dealt to the Oshawa Generals, where—handsome, articulate, and a violent dream on the ice—he had no problem living up to his billing. And, it doesn't hurt to note that the league, as a result of Eric's situation, instituted a number of changes to reduce travel time for its players.

Eric's very success, though, led to the next patch of rough ice for the Lindros family.

It was 1991 and Quebec had the first pick overall in the NHL Entry Draft. Even before the draft, Eric made it clear he would not play for the Nordiques. Again, the Lindroses made the decision as a family. They had talked to players, agents, and others who were familiar with the team's ownership, and Eric decided it wasn't the right situation for him. "The chances of that organization ever having a winning team were remote," Eric explains. "It wasn't the type of team I wanted to play for."

Like the Sault Ste. Marie Greyhounds in the Canadian junior league, the team thought the family was bluffing and drafted Eric. And, again, the family held firm in its decision. A player fighting to have some control over where he would play just didn't happen in

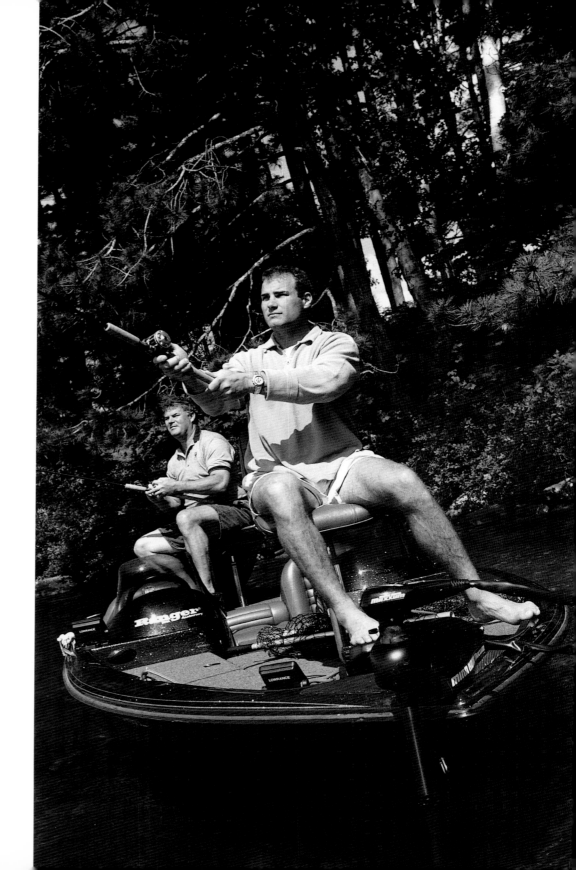

the NHL in those days, even after years as a pro. (In hockey, free agency isn't an option until age 31.) Rather than play for Quebec, Eric simply withdrew his availability. He returned to junior hockey and played for the Canadian National Team in the 1992 Olympics.

As a result, the Lindros family felt the scorn of a large segment of hockey purists for the second time in Eric's career, and he wasn't yet 20 years old. Buck the system? Buck the old-school methods of the NHL?

"We did what we thought was right," Eric emphasizes again. And, "what was allowed by NHL rules," his father adds.

Just before the 1992–1993 season, with the Nordiques trying to salvage something out of their first-round pick, they traded Eric to the Philadelphia Flyers for six players, two first-round draft picks, and $15 million. The Flyers had called the Lindroses before making the trade, and sitting with his father in a cramped bedroom at the family's cottage, Eric agreed to what would become a six-year contract for $21 million. (The deal worked out for the Flyers, too. In 1997, Eric, the team captain, led them to the Stanley Cup Finals.). As if to prove Eric's concerns about the Nordiques, they actually traded him to two teams at once—the Flyers and the New York Rangers. While that mess was being untangled by league officials, the family made another difficult decision—that Carl would represent Eric. Tired of what they saw as the manipulations of agents, Eric asked his father to take care of his business dealings. Carl initially declined, but later changed his mind and withdrew as a partner in Canada's largest public accounting and consulting firm to help Eric.

"It's perfect," says Eric, dismissing the idea that mixing family and business can add stress rather than diminish it. "Dad handles the contracts, the endorsements, the business proposals, taxes, I mean making sure my insurance is in place. It's a full-time affair. You pick up the phone and there are times when it's business and times when it's not—and now that they have these satellites up, Dad has a few things to say about kicking my game up a notch. But business is business, and I have the benefit of being able to trust my father. There's no reason for tension."

Later, Carl would also represent his son Brett, and perhaps the biggest benefit of having a father in that position was realized soon after the younger Lindros joined the NHL.

Brett, physical like his older brother but lacking his size, was drafted ninth overall in the first round of the 1994 NHL Entry Draft by the New York Islanders. He was scrappy, tough, and talented on the ice, and he would still be considered valuable to most NHL teams. "I like the good, hard, clean check," he says with words that could be attributed to his brother. "I like the fight if it's necessary."

The fight of his life, though, would finally take him out of professional hockey. It was an ongoing battle, really, with concussions. With each succeeding blow to the head, it seemed, the concussions would come easier and be more severe than the last. The final injury came simply from decelerating on his skates. Finally, after a season-and-a-half in the NHL, he took the advice of three specialists and said good-bye to his hockey career.

"It got to the point," explains his father, "where there was a real risk of serious, permanent injury."

Carl agreed with his son that the risk was not worth the money, the glory, not worth anything. "I could see a lot of agents going, 'Oh, man, one of my players just retired—I just lost my 4 percent," says Brett. "My dad decided to watch out for me and for others."

The following is a letter from Tim Cohn about his relationship with his father, Ed Cohn, the commissioner for the Indiana Department of Corrections. Father and son were estranged for years, with Tim getting into trouble with drugs and the law. Repeatedly, he grasped the helping hand of his father, only to slap it away when he felt he was on his feet. But he would slip again. Finally, he had a moment in his father's office that changed both of their lives forever—more troubles notwithstanding. Tim was born 6-6-66, in Gary, Indiana.

Mom was a gregarious drinker twenty years ahead of her time. Dad was a stoic sports fanatic who sometimes seemed emotionally unavailable. They were both very intelligent and at some point feared for the neurotic genius they named Tim.

My folks trudged through an ugly divorce when I was 13. That was the first year I made little league all-stars, but somehow it seemed empty. I lived three tumultuous years with my mother, aging far beyond my years in a short amount of time. My father and I did not speak. He closeted the Christmas presents he'd sent and I'd returned.

We had lost the innocence of a father and son bond. Time and again he would offer help and I'd refuse, but I appreciated his attempts to restore some semblance of a normal childhood just the same. As I got older, he encouraged me to put my energies into extracurricular activities at school instead of continuing to work three jobs. These activities included football. I had a good GPA and a great SAT score. I was recruited to play by some academically sound schools. I started at Wabash College.

I never really applied myself at Wabash or any of the several other schools that followed. I was, however, pretty good at selling dope and a few other illegal activities Dad would never have approved of. At the height of my outlaw days, my dad sensed I was in trouble. He pushed the issue and threatened fisticuffs. I retreated within myself, and he realized a sound thrashing would

not bring me around. I remember the day I went to his office (at the time he was the superintendent at the state reformatory). I passed security and headed into the imposing tomb where he worked. We were at odds, at our worst. I expected an ultimatum or a slap, but what I got was Dad saying, "Son, I love you. I know you're not where you want to be. I just want you to know that I support you and whatever it is you want to be, I love you." He got up from behind his imposing desk and hugged me. I was 19 years old and the tears streamed down my cheeks as I heard those words for the first time from my father's mouth.

Soon after that I left the state to continue my pseudo-collegiate career in Louisiana. He cut me off financially because I was doing poorly at school or not attending at all. I continued to flounder. To stay in school I joined the National Guard. He was relieved if not proud. There was a certain semblance of, "It'll make a man out of you" to it.

I got activated to go to Desert Storm. I eloped on the way over there and came home with a wife. From 1991, when I returned home and my marriage failed, to 1996, I didn't have much contact with Dad. I would call only in times of eviction to ask for money.

In 1997, I was passing through Indianapolis from New Orleans while tour managing a band on its way to Chicago, so I stopped to see him. Not much had changed. He was still Dad, and he still loved me, despite my actions. Shortly thereafter I was contracted to host and perform spoken word—a form of poetry—at Peace in the Park, a music festival in Indianapolis. It was a big show for me and I was nervous. Dad was scheduled to be there in the evening, but he showed up early and a jazz band showed up late. The promoter asked me to fill thirty minutes.

I went up and did my set. I rocked. Dad saw me backstage with four people thanking me and asking for autographs (no small feat for a poet at a rock show). He joked with the promoter, saying that he had written all my materi-

al. Later, he said that he realized how hard a job I was trying to do and that he was proud of me. I never thought I would ever live to hear those words.

When I was a kid, I always had access to convicts for school papers and interviews. My interviewees never knew who I was. I suppose they consented to my presence without questioning how I got it. In all the interviews I did, I always baited the inmates to talk negatively about the warden. What I always heard back was that he was a straight shooter, that he might not say what they wanted to hear, but that he always told it like it was. There were times when I did not like my dad or even understand him, but in talking to people who worked for him or were incarcerated in his jails, I learned to respect him. I think he's always known that. I hope he has.

—Tim

Ed Cohn knew he had a troubled son. He wasn't so sure how to react. The hardest part, he says, was when he watched Tim fall into trouble time and again. He didn't want to step in too soon, too forcefully. He feared that by pushing into Tim's life, he would push him away. It's one of the toughest parts of parenting, he reflects, this knowing when to step in and knowing when to step away.

"We can make mistakes, but we have an opportunity to learn from them and grow from them," he explains, sitting in his Indianapolis office, where he makes a living overseeing a population that has made serious mistakes. "I think there's always a concern when anybody in the family goes left of center. For me, there was the added, 'What's this going to mean to me professionally?' But the bigger concern was whether he was okay, what's going on with him."

There were nights Ed Cohn would lay in bed, wondering what had become of his son. Sometimes he didn't know what Tim was up to. Sometimes he wasn't even sure what state Tim was in. He took the "no

news is good news" tact. It wasn't just a philosophy that was forced on him by the circumstances. It was a survival tool.

"I would have much rather have had a phone call every week or so from him during that time, but on the other hand I thought, okay, I'm not getting a call from some agency or a priest or a rabbi, he must be okay," Ed recalls. "It was painful for me. But I think it would have hurt me and him more if I would have placed myself in a position that he didn't want me to be in. Had I pushed at the wrong time too hard, that could have hurt things in the future."

So what's a father to do? His instinct is to protect his child—even if it means throttling him by the neck. On the other hand, kids grow up. Sometimes the road to adulthood is smooth. Sometimes it's not.

The key is distinguishing between a rough road and one that is leading to nowhere but trouble. Ed's approach was to wait, watch, hope for the best, and let Tim know that he didn't have to travel the road alone.

"The important thing was he knew that when he was ready, I'd be there," Ed says. "It's not always easy being a father. I think fatherhood . . .I don't think there's anything that can compare to it. Professionally, I've been very successful, but I don't think there's anything more meaningful than being a dad, watching a kid grow up, helping him grow up.

"I like to have him around," he continues. "At the same time, I know he has his own life and that ability to achieve. I wouldn't want him totally dependent on me or a wife or some social agency. I don't ever worry about Tim surviving. If I'm no longer around, and he doesn't have me to call, he'll be able to survive. He's smart, he's astute, and he'll be able to make it. He's a survivor."

Tim Cohn reconciled with his mother, Mary Kathleen Boyle, before her death. He is working in the movie and concert industries. He and his father see each other often.

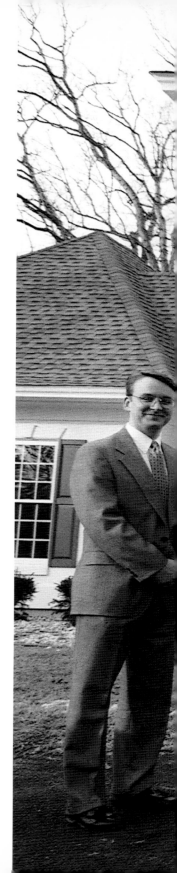

The Diamonds: Eugene, Gene, Peter, Terrence, Brian, Sean, Mark, and Timothy

First, let's go to the numbers. Dr. Eugene Diamond has been married since 1950. He has seven sons, thirteen children total. He has fifty-two grandchildren. Among his sons, five are doctors, two are lawyers. Of his daughters, two are social workers, one is a physical therapist, one is a nurse, one is a lawyer, and the other is in science administration.

Not a bad legacy for a guy whose own father died when he was six, in the middle of the Great Depression, leaving behind five children and no money.

Diamond built his own success the old-fashioned way: He went to war for it. A Navy corpsman in World War II, he used the G.I. Bill to put himself through medical school and build a successful pediatric practice. He and his wife, Rosemary, never intended to have so many children. That's just the way it went. "In fact," says Diamond in his suburban Chicago home, "early in our marriage we had a tough time having kids. There were miscarriages, problems. We were concerned about just how big a family we'd have. But

The Diamonds, from left, Mark, Sean, Peter, Gene, Eugene, Terry, Tim, and Brian.

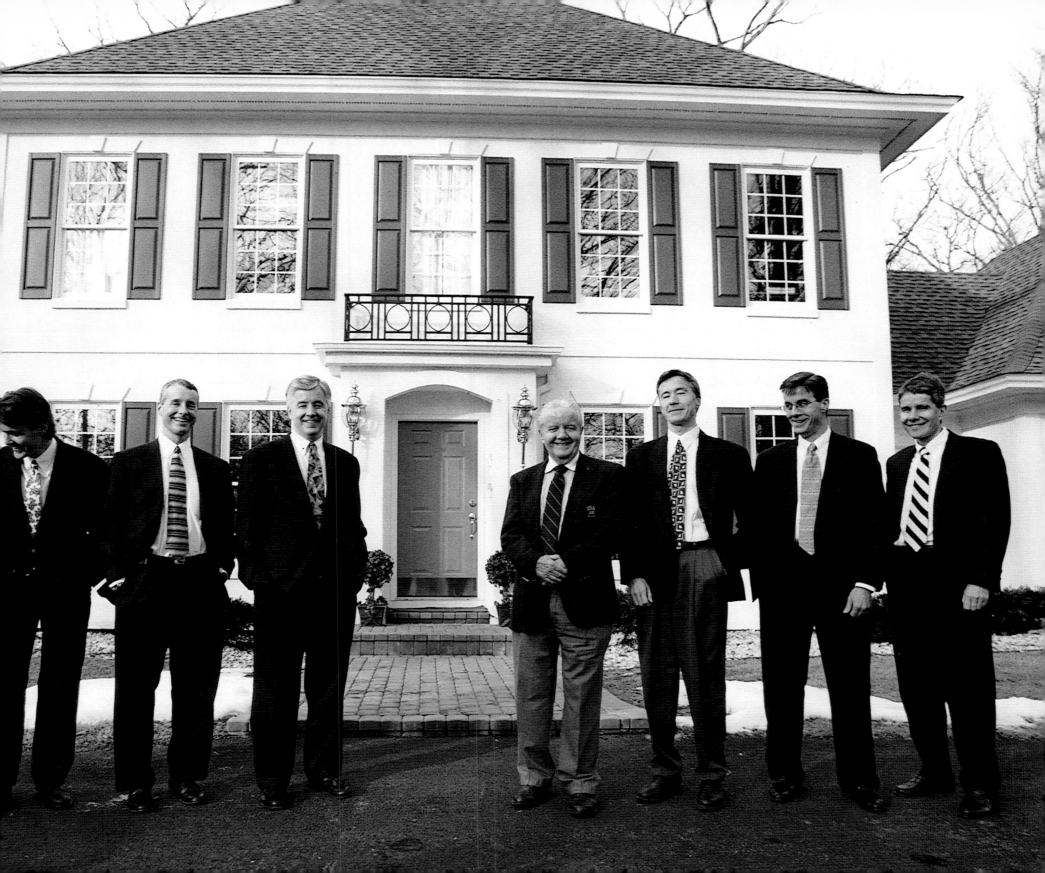

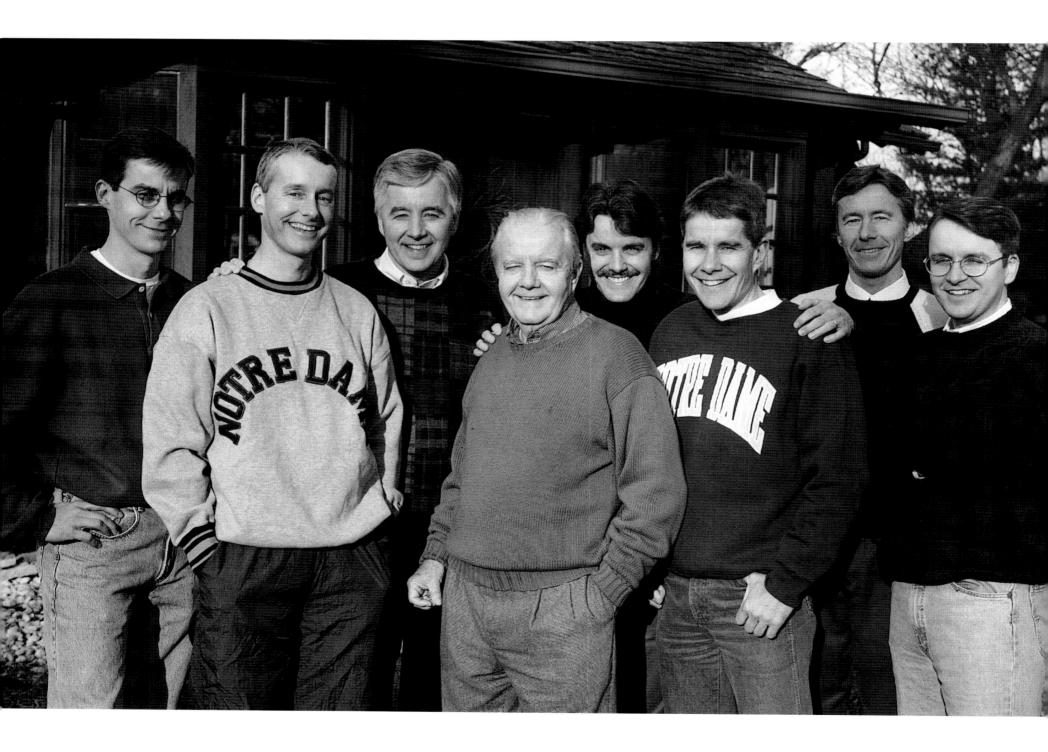

once that first olive got out of the bottle . . ."

The rest is family history. In addition to his daughters, the father had Gene Christopher, 47, Peter Sean, 46, Terrence Patrick, 44, Brian James, 43, Sean Michael, 42, Mark Damian, 41, and Timothy Joseph, 35. (Yes, they are Irish Catholic.) At one point, Diamond had five children in pre-school at the same time. Which was nothing compared to the financial strains he would face later: putting all of his children through college, five of his sons through medical school, and the other two through law school. (At one point or another, all of the sons and all but two of the daughters attended Notre Dame.)

How did they manage? "I don't want to overstate things and say it was Spartan self-denial, but it meant certain luxuries were out, things that other physicians had I wouldn't have," Diamond recalls, still working well into his seventies. "What you invest in your family is not necessarily a sacrifice. It's an investment in their future and in your future. I have no feeling that I performed any kind of heroic sacrifice. I've benefited as much as my children have."

Sean, though, the fifth son, a pediatrician, doesn't quite buy that, not with four kids of his own. "One of the things that we all feel as we each add a few more gray hairs is the sacrifice both he and my mother made," he says. "With him being the sole breadwinner while raising thirteen kids . . . we get a little more respect for him as we see how hard it is to raise our own kids." Adds Brian, the fourth son, a malpractice attorney: "He had a poor upbringing. He'd tell us these stories, and they'd be really funny stories, but we'd glean from them how bad he had it, so it's not lost on any of us how much he sacrificed."

There was the time, for example, during the Depression, where Diamond's mother scraped together enough money for a pot roast. It was a rarity for the family and when the roast was set out for a second,

the dog took off with the meat. "My father's telling this story and he just puts on this unbelievable face and tells us, 'Everyone was going Aggghhh!'" recalls Brian. "To see his face, we couldn't help but laugh, and he wanted to make us laugh, but we understood where he had come from."

Soon after Diamond got married he had more than money to worry about. With a wife and six daughters how does a father give the proper attention to seven sons? How does he merely get them safely into adulthood—let alone help them to become thriving professionals?

One way was to insist on a family meal every night, regardless of who had baseball practice or when the father would finally get home from a long day at the office. "We always ate together," recalls Gene, the eldest son, an attorney and chief executive officer of St. Margaret's Hospital in the Chicago suburb of Hammond. "Especially our dinner meals. We'd eat at 7:30-8:00 sometimes, because it was important to him, and to my mother, that we sit down and eat as a family. There were to be no excuses."

"Meals may have been one way," Diamond says, "but oftentimes I'd take them out in pairs. We'd do things as a family, but other things, I'd think it best to just take a couple of them. There wasn't enough one-on-one, I know that. But when they were going through particularly stressful periods, then I'd kind of single them out for more attention." An added help is inherent to large families. That is, soon teenagers are helping to take care of their toddler siblings. It puts responsibility on the teenager and it keeps another set of eyes on the younger ones. "The relationship between children in a large family, particularly between an adolescent and a pre-school sibling is such a rich, rich thing. Everybody benefits from it," he says.

"Maybe that's a reason none of us really rebelled," adds Mark, son number six, an internist. "I mean, everybody in their own way kind of rebelled, but nothing too major, and it was always within the family." The father remembers, for instance, the time Mark was on the high school track team and Peter bought him an expensive pair of running shoes. Mark wanted to show them off, wearing them at school. "I told him 'You can't do that, they should be reserved for track meets and practice,'" Diamond recalls. "He said, 'Well, they're my shoes and you can't tell me what to do with them.' I said, 'Okay, if you say so.' That night when he went to sleep, I absconded with the shoes. It was kind of an extended banging of the heads, but the important thing is, it wasn't about the shoes for me. It was about who's in charge."

Says Peter, son number two, a cardiologist: "With so many of us and the relationships we had, the sibling rivalry just would not allow one or the other of us to fly too far out of line. We're not afraid to tell each other when we're being jerks." Adds Timothy, son number seven, an attorney: "In a family our size, you always had someone to play with. On the other side, there was always someone who knew what was going on with you."

All of the sons say their father was a strict disciplinarian whose tactics did not always endear him to his children. He did not allow his kids to go out to drink beer with their buddies when they were growing up. Dating was forbidden until age 16; going steady was discouraged until the sons and daughters were well into college. Curfews in high school were midnight on the weekends. "My dad was never afraid of being unpopular with his kids," says Mark. "I think he had a pretty good idea of what kind of kids he wanted. That didn't make him popular with us, especially at different times, but he wasn't hypocritical. I remember in high school going face-to-face with him and screaming and yelling, but I'd realize he wasn't telling us not to go out with our friends and get in trouble on a Friday night, then sit around and booze it up himself."

"Most of what he taught us, he taught us by example," says Brian, recalling how his father would leave for the office early in the morning, return late in the evening, and never utter a word of complaint. "He worked hard; we saw that. He's a very smart guy, and driven, too, and it was always expected that we would be successful on some grand kind of scale. Since we were knee-high, we knew we were going to college. There just wasn't any other way. He went to college. That was an example."

"He's still that way," adds Terry, the third son, a pulminologist. "He still stresses that we're professionals, we had the education, and we should be an example to others. I think in that sense, my dad was so consistent and had so much fortitude, we could almost have taken on a kind of cynicism, like, 'I can't be like that guy, why even try?'"

All seven sons did try, however, and they all succeeded. Now that they are adults, their respect for their father has only grown and the brothers have become even closer to each other. To Diamond, that is his greatest achievement. "They're very, very close," he says. "Small families tend to be intensive, and they tend to concentrate on the community; as with a large family, siblings tend to choose each other as their best friends." If it sounds as though the doctor has noted enough observations to fill a book, well, he has. The Large Family: A Blessing and a Challenge is filled with his observations on how to raise a large family, the obstacles parents face, and the rewards that are in the offing.

"I wrote it, of course, to be of some help," Diamond says. "But I think true, good parenting comes from within. I think accepting parenthood can be a natural thing that doesn't have to have any pre-ordained rules. I wasn't preoccupied with consulting the experts on how I should or should not raise my children, and I think that was a secret to my success. For me, it came simply out of love for the child."

The Alomars: Sandy, Sandy Jr., and Roberto

From left, the Alomars: Sandy, Roberto, and Sandy, Jr. at Cleveland's Jacobs Field.

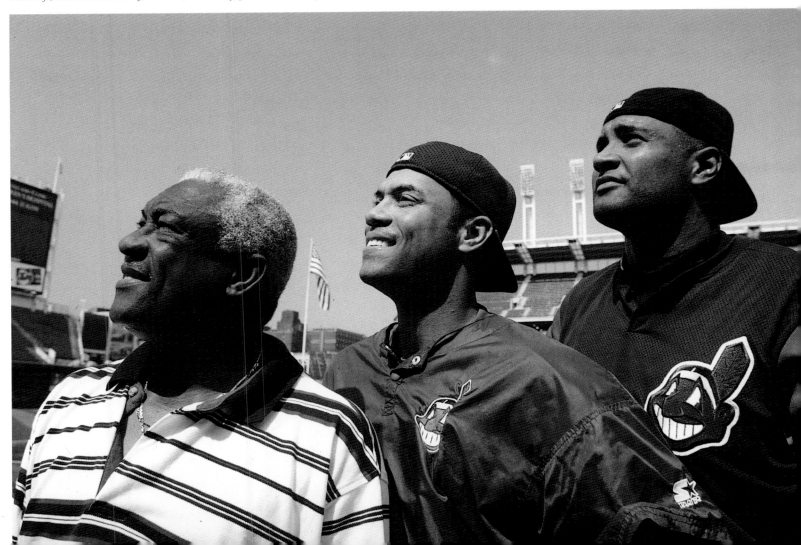

Sandy Alomar Jr. and his brother, Roberto, still get tears in their eyes from laughing about their time at the ballpark when they were kids and their father, Sandy Sr., was playing professional baseball.

There were the days in the Puerto Rican winter league, for example, when Sandy Jr. stole the catcher's glove from Luis Isaac just before Issac was supposed to return to the field. "Where's my glove? Where's my glove?" Isaac would yell, and players would laugh and umpires would get impatient and Sandy Jr. and his little brother would play catch in the bullpen, using Isaac's glove until he finally caught up with them.

And then there was that time Roberto—Robbie, as he is known—used a stick and a rock as a bat and a ball and blasted a line drive smack into Isaac's lip. The two were in the bullpen at a ballpark in Puerto Rico, and Isaac chased Robbie, then about 12, until he had him cornered. With nowhere to go but up, Robbie scaled the bullpen fence and hopped to the other side. Unfortunately for him, he landed on the field during a game. The umpires called time out. Robbie froze. Isaac grabbed Robbie.

The two brothers are reliving these stories inside the third-base dugout of Jacobs Field, home of the Cleveland Indians, and all the while, sitting between them, is their father, a second baseman for several clubs when his sons were pulling their antics. Sandy Sr. is enjoying his visit with his sons, both of whom made it to the big leagues and became stars themselves. He sits between them, listens, smiles and then laughs when Robbie busts up his brother. Isaac, now a bullpen coach with the Indians, busts up too.

"Louie's lip was bleeding—" Robbie tries to finish the story but can't, he is laughing so hard, sitting on the bench, leaning to his side, holding his stomach with both hands.

"Got you, didn't I?" Louie finishes with a big grin.

Sandy Sr. rubs his hand from his forehead to his neck, shaking his head, remembering the stories and laughing with his sons and old teammate.

And why shouldn't he?

These are the happiest of days for the Alomar family. Almost any father dreams of his sons loving baseball, a sport with a special history and a special charm. Fathers coach their kids in little league, take them to their first ball games, teach them how to keep score, how to compute a pitcher's earned run average. They reminisce about how peanuts used to cost a quarter and about how great the sport was when Bob Feller was pitching or when Mickey Mantle and Hank Aaron were belting home runs. They tease their sons with that classic "Who's on First?" routine.

Not only did the Alomar brothers take to the game, they took it by storm. From humble roots in the middle-class town of Salinas, Puerto Rico, all three Alomars rose to become Major League Baseball stars. The father, an all-star, played for several teams from 1964 to 1978, including the 1976 American League champion New York Yankees. He is now a roving coach for the Chicago Cubs, tutoring minor leaguers. A keen evaluator of baseball talent, Sandy Sr. saw his sons' potential early in life and hoped they would make it to the bigs. When they did, though, he almost dreaded the games his boys would play against each other. Sandy, a catcher for the Indians, would play several times a season against Robbie, a second baseman for the Baltimore Orioles.

Twice, in 1996 and 1997, they faced each other in the playoffs.

"I was always rooting for both of them," Sandy Sr. says. "I wanted

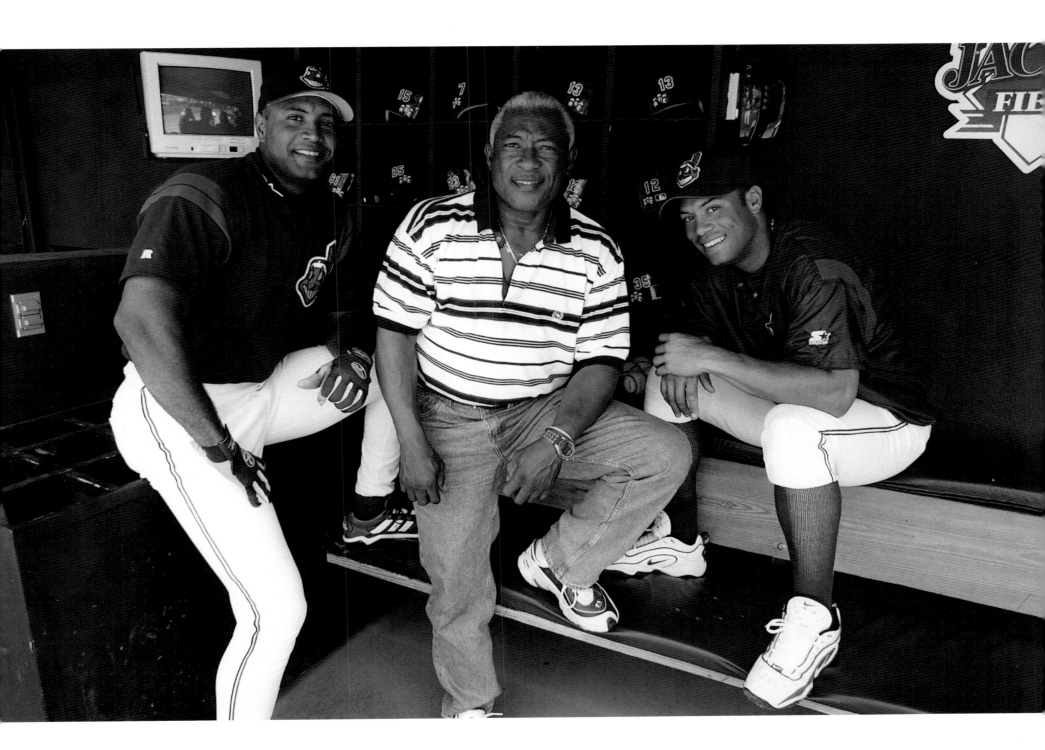

them both to do well." And the Alomar brothers have done very well, giving their father much to cheer about. Both are repeat all-stars and have nearly a dozen Gold Gloves between them. When Robbie was named Most Valuable Player in the 1998 all-star game, one year after his brother won the honor, they became the first brothers in Major League history to accomplish the feat. And, not coincidentally, their respective teams have done well too. It has been said that the Alomars are to October what the Kennedys are to November—never in the 1990s was there a post-season in the American League without an Alomar in the lineup.

While proud of his sons' individual accomplishments, the successes of their ballclubs presented Sandy Sr. with a dilemma. "I couldn't root for one team or the other," he says, "because then it was like I was rooting against one of them."

When the younger Alomars broke into the league a decade ago, rooting against one of his sons wasn't an issue for their father. Sandy Jr. and Robbie both played for the San Diego Padres, and when they'd look down the third-base line from the batters box, Sandy Sr. was in the coaches box, flashing them the signs. (The organist used to play the theme from "All in Family" when either brother was batting.) But Sandy Jr. was traded to the Indians later that year and the Padres sent Robbie to the Toronto Blue Jays and then he went to the Orioles. Not until the 1999 season would the brothers be reunited, this time in Cleveland.

"Now it's nice," Sandy Sr. says. "Now I can root for the team to win." And, with the Alomars in the lineup, the Indians have won. They have given Cleveland reliable offense and defense, and they have given each other—and their father—a little extra comfort on the field and off.

"When we were kids we wanted to play together in the big leagues," Robbie says. "It's like a dream come true to play together. We're taking advantage of it, trying to have fun and helping each other."

Football and basketball may rival baseball for popularity these days, but there is no more endearing image than a father and son having a simple catch with each other. That ritual started young for the Alomar brothers. They played baseball with their father growing up in Salinas, and, for the most part, they've played baseball ever since.

"Robbie had a ball from the time before he could start walking—from before then," his father remembers. "That's all he ever wanted to do." Robbie begins laughing again when he recalls just how much he loved to be at the ballpark, any ballpark.

"My dad was going to the game and he didn't want me to go," Robbie explains. "He was going to San Juan, and I hid in the back of the station wagon. I popped up an hour later—'Hi, Dad.' He had to just keep going. That's how bad I wanted to be at the game."

Robbie's love for the game would be tested in 1996 in an ugly incident that could have obscured his successes had it not been for those Gold Gloves and clutch bat. The incident was this: Alomar spit on an umpire. He apologized for it, donated money to charity to help make amends, but for a long time he was booed in parks all across the American League. It was tough for a guy with such an easy grin to be seen as a villain, but the experience also demonstrated to him again that his father had more than just batting signs and fielding tips to pass on to him.

"He said, 'It's tough but simple. Keep your head up, be the person you are, play the game the way you play the game,'" Robbie says.

"We're human beings and we're always going to make mistakes."

Sandy Jr. never faced such wrath at any level of baseball, but he has never been as infatuated with the game as his little brother. In fact, he quit baseball between his twelfth and fourteenth birthdays, a crucial time in the development of a ball player. He wanted to race his dirt bike. Then his father sat him down and explained that riding a bike was a hobby, not a job.

"But he let us make our own decisions," Sandy Jr. says, adding that such allowances went beyond career choices, extending into life choices. "He' s not the type of guy who will overwhelm you. He'd say, 'If you're going to do something, do it right. And do it in front of me, not behind my back.' Whatever we did was going to be okay—as long as we didn't do drugs or something like that."

Sandy Sr. is shy about taking credit for the way his sons turned out. Beyond their talent on the field, both are loved in Cleveland for their easy personalities and for being actively involved in a number of charities. Robbie's incident is well behind him. As far Sandy Sr.'s concerned, he's just a lucky father.

"I never had to be too strict with them," Sandy Sr. says. "A lot of it had to do with baseball. If they were acting up, I took away their gloves. That's all I had to do. As far as their joking around goes," he adds with a smile, "there's nothing I want to do about that."

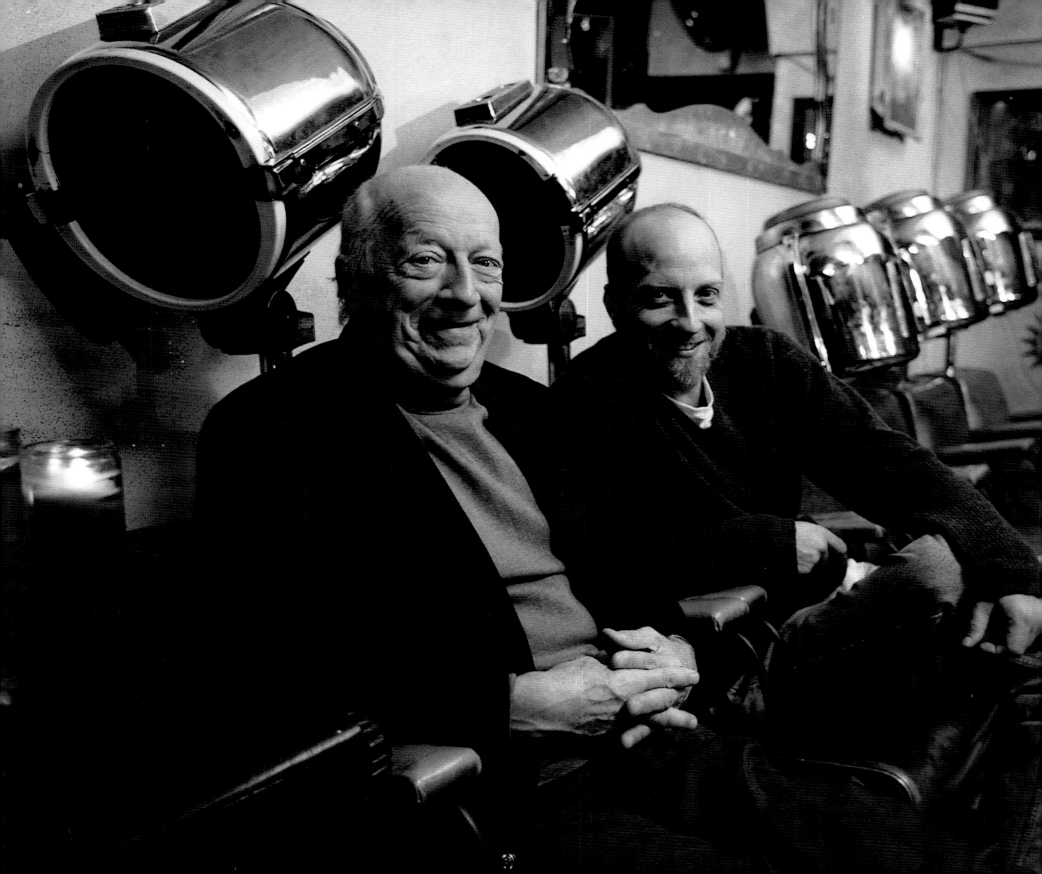

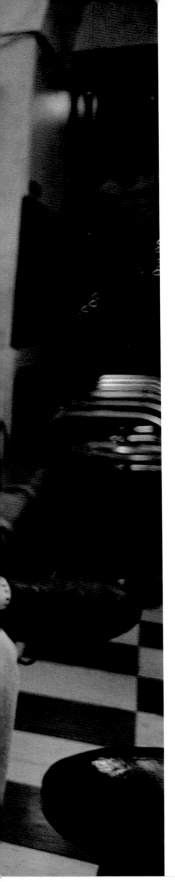

The Elliotts: Bob and Chris

I t was 1981, and David Letterman and his mom, Dorothy, were doing some sightseeing in New York. Letterman's morning television show had just been canceled, and he was preparing to claim the 12:30 AM slot following Johnny Carson. He and his mother approached the ticket window for the observation deck of the World Trade Center.

Behind the glass, selling the tickets, was a ham named Chris Elliott. Recognizing Letterman from his frequent stints filling in for Carson on the *Tonight Show*, and seeing he was with his mother, Elliott rang up the total for the man who was getting ready to invent a whole new brand of late-night talk show. He charged him the kiddy price.

"And then I immediately blurted out who my dad was," recalls Elliott, his father, Bob Elliott, sitting to his side. "Dave says, 'Oh, yeah, I'm a huge fan of his.' He said, 'When I host the *Tonight Show*, I'm always trying to get him on.' I said, 'Yeah, well he only does the *Tonight Show* when Johnny's on.' Looking back, maybe

Bob Elliot and his son Chris joke at Manhattan's Beauty Bar.

cast, Letterman needed someone to wear a garbage suit for a comedy bit, and Chris volunteered. As his father had said, he became part of the mix. Soon he was writing for the show (winning four Emmy Awards for it) and getting increased on-air time, pushing his comedy to the limits his father knew so well, always getting his biggest laughs just as his skits threatened to go irretrievably overboard.

"The thing is, on that show at that time, we felt we could string people along absolutely as far as possible before they'd finally get it," Chris recalls. "We had a feeling nobody was watching in the first place, and the people who were watching deserved to be strung along. If it wasn't for Dave, I don't know where I could have cut a niche. It was the perfect show for it."

As close to the edge as their comedy often is, the father and son could not be more centered. The most striking thing about them when they're not performing is just how normal they are. Chris, whose characters are often sincere in the most insincere, smarmy ways, talks about his father's influence like any son who has a father he admires. He throws an arm around his father's shoulder, mugs for his dad because he knows he'll get a laugh. Bob, whose characters were often oblivious to the realities around them, laughs at every aside his son makes, nods in agreement at every point he pushes. Chris does the same back.

Despite Bob's legend and the obvious appreciation for each other's work, the two don't sit around and dissect comedy. "There's always been this sort of unspoken rule not to talk specifics about our various ends of the business," says Chris. "It would never occur to me to ask him about how a joke is structured. Maybe because it's almost an embarrassment that we have about what we do for a living, and maybe talking about it gives it more seriousness than it deserves."

Which does not mean they are beyond playing off each other. In *Daddy's Boy*, a 1989 book written by Chris with alternating rebuttals by Bob, Chris harps on the hell of being a celebrity's son. In the memoir, the satirist's answer to "Mommy Dearest," an abused Chris shows photos of how, as a boy, he was forced to wear a Latex bald wig because his tyrannical father demanded they look alike. Chris goes through the humiliation he suffered in his "fatty years," when he was toted to school in a crane. And he agonizes over that painful period in his life when his father—obsessed with Gold-Toe socks—insisted that Chris also wear them, always.

The Elliots' repartee was never so obvious as when they worked together on *Get a Life*. "The funny thing that happened to me was how people would ask, 'Who played your dad?'" Chris says. "And I was like, 'Oh, that's my dad'. When we were shooting the pilot, I had in the back of my mind that he'd be perfect for the part, but you know, we both had kind of this aversion to Hollywood. I was really happy when he said yes, because when we finished the pilot, there was nobody else who could do it in my mind.

"It worked out great," he continues. "I was glad to cash in on my dad's fame once again. I'm unbelievably proud of him and I'd be a fan of his even if I weren't his son. One thing I realize is I've been cashing in on who my dad is for a long time, both in terms of learning from him and tossing his name around to people like Letterman. It's something I'm extremely proud of."

His father, in pure affection, rolls his eyes and fakes a slap to his own forehead and in a dry, serious look turns to Chris.

"We've got about two hours left for this interview," he says, knowing they have to leave in minutes. "Go ahead and keep talking about how great I am."

The Hoffs: Thomas, Ray, and Bob

From left, brothers Ray and Bob Hoff at the firehouse in Chicago's Chinatown.

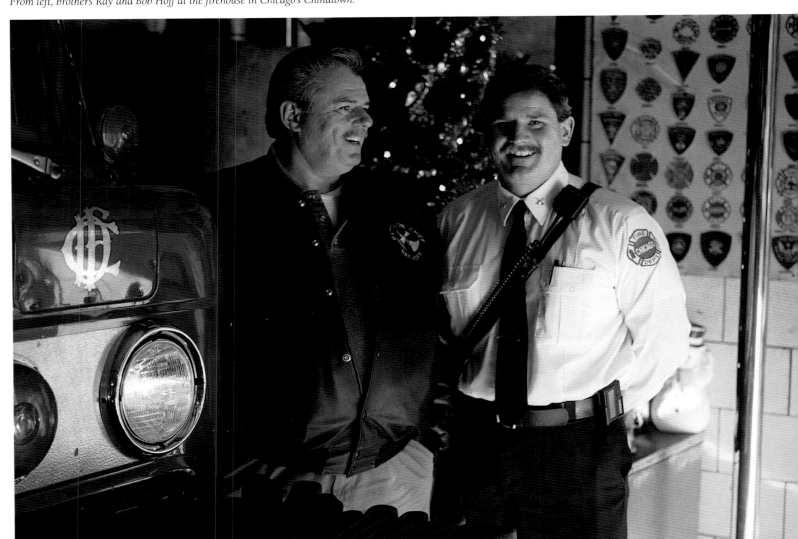

It was Valentine's Day, 1966. Bob Hoff was home from school, sick with the measles, when the telephone in his Chicago home started to ring off the hook. He was only 6, but he could sense something was wrong. Ray Hoff was 20 years old and working seven stories up at the Illinois Central Railroad; he had a good view of the fire that was raging a few blocks away. Then his boss came into his office and told him he should go home, that there had been an accident.

Their father, Battalion Chief Thomas Hoff, had been killed at 44. He was fighting a fire when the roof gave way. Rescuers searched for hours before they found him, both sons on the scene by then, the little one wearing his father's fire helmet when the body was recovered. Their loss was compounded six years later, when their mother died.

It was their father's death, though, that would nearly kill the sons.

The movie *Backdraft* was drawn largely from the story of the Hoffs—Thomas, Ray, and Bob—as well as the first firefighter in the family, their grandfather, Joseph. (Joseph fought the 1910 stockyards blaze that took the lives of twenty-one firefighters, the department's worst single loss of life.) Ray is now retired, Bob now the Battalion chief in Chicago's Chinatown. Many men who lose their fathers at a young age will tell you that despite the distance that death renders, their relationship with their fathers continues to evolve long after their passing. Feelings change when the sons hit the milestones they only vaguely remember their fathers hitting—if they remember them at all. The first big career decision, marriage, buying a first home, having a child, all of those things alter the perceptions the sons once had of their fathers. At those junctures, the father becomes real again.

But for Ray and Bob Hoff, the distance between them and their father would never be much farther away than the flames that would flick around them at their next fire. Both of them, after their father's death, would ride the firetrucks in their neighborhood. Both of them would become firemen. And both of them would nearly die as their father died.

"When you have a death in the family like that, you can't help but think of it when you go on a call," says Ray. "For me, that was both a blessing and a curse."

Ray was injured fifteen times in fires during his first three years on the job, which, as planned before that fateful Valentine's Day, he took eight months after his father's death. "It took me a while to figure it out. It took some counseling sessions," he explains. "What I finally realized was, psychologically, when I was fighting these fires, I think it was an 'I'm going to go in and get my father out' kind of thing. I think it made me go into places I probably shouldn't have gone. It's just . . . fire became my personal enemy, the thing that had taken my father. There was a compensation thing going."

Then the most frightening thought hit him: "I came to realize," he says, "that for me to feel full, somebody had to be in trouble. That really disturbed me because it was like, am I performing a service for the public by saving them from fires or are they performing a service for me by letting me do it? When that hit me, that's when I started to level off with it."

Ray had dozens of stitches and plenty of sprains to show for the problems connected to his father's death. Bob had a few injuries of his own, mostly minor—for a while. Then another death nearly hit the family. Bob was fighting a fire in 1984. He was picking through a roof, trying to ventilate the attic. There was a flash of flames. They snapped at him. Singed him. There was no water to fight them. A decision: Jump through a window, 2½ stories high? Or take a chance and run through the flames? He ran through the flames. He still has the scars on his back to remind him of that day, not that a reminder is necessary. He was burned on over 30 percent of his body. He spent a month in the hospital.

"It was a humbling experience," he says. "It woke me up big time not to be so aggressive. You know, you fight fires, fight fires, and it becomes second nature to you, and you can get a little cocky. Believe me, I learned. I wouldn't wish it on anybody to get burned. The pain you're in is unbelievable. My head was the size of a basketball. I couldn't open my eyes for four days. Morphine was like nothing at all. I'm not being melodramatic, or don't mean to be, but I remember more than a couple of times I wanted to run my head into a brick wall."

Neither their father's death nor Bob's injuries, though, caused either brother to go easy on fires. Just a bit more cautiously. "Sure, I think his death had something to do with me putting myself into some positions I shouldn't have been in," Bob admits. "It's something like, he'd want me to be the best fireman ever, and putting myself into some of those positions did that, even if it shouldn't have."

Twice, Bob has received the Chicago Fire Department's highest award for bravery. The first award came after he rescued an elderly couple from their home on Chicago's North Side after a gas explosion. The second award came about when he was returning from a fire at a vacant building. He got a call about a house fire. When he pulled up, a woman was screaming that two 4-year-old boys were trapped on the second floor.

The boys were twins, and their bedroom was across the hall from a kitchen that was engulfed in flames. The first firefighter on the scene, Bob rushed in, fought heavy smoke in a stairwell and flames rolling across the hallway ceiling. One child he found under a comforter. The other was beneath a pile of clothes. They were unconscious. When Hoff got them outside, he administered CPR. They survived.

"It makes you feel good any time you can help somebody," Bob Hoff says. "There's a balancing act, a very tough one, that goes on. You're looking out for other people, but you have to look out for yourself, too. There are chances you take, but you minimize the risks by knowing what you're doing, and you know what you're doing through good training."

Minimizing risks and saving lives has not brought closure to either brother, however. Their father and grandfather are gone now, and no number of rescues is going to change that, as tidy as that would be. Instead, they carry on and make the best of horrible situations by traveling the country, spreading their family's story, and discussing the dangers they themselves have faced. They teach technical lessons, but they try to teach life lessons as well.

"I've had time to think about what would I want to leave behind, as in a legacy," Ray explains, "and I decided if you've learned something, you should pass it on. My father always told me, 'Don't forget where you came from on this job. When you go to work, hug your significant other and your children, and when you come home, do the same thing again.' It was good advice before I became a fireman, and it's good advice now."

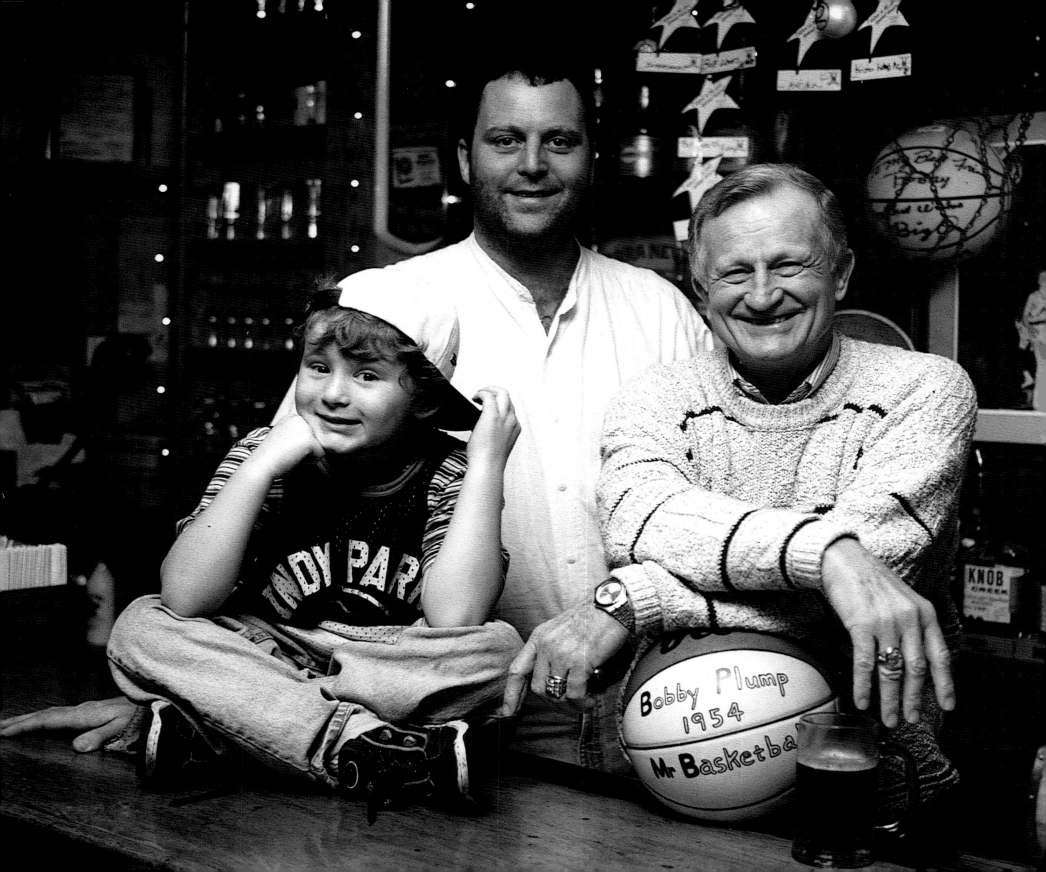

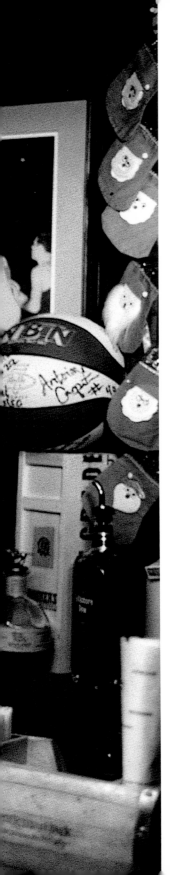

The Plumps: Bobby, Jonathan, and Garrett

Tick . . . tick . . . tick . . .

The seconds snap by. When the horn sounds, one skinny little kid from the plains will be the biggest hero in Indiana—ever. Or he will be the goat who blew it—big time. It is 1954. Tiny Milan High School is playing the giants from Muncie Central, the eight-time state champions, the beefy acrobats who everyone knows will slam-dunk the upstart challengers into oblivion. Everyone knows it but Milan, that is. Anybody with a pulse in Indiana is watching the game either in person or on television, or listening to it on the radio, and they are more than surprised. Hearts are pounding as hard as the feet stomping on the wooden bleachers.

Little Milan, you see, is more than holding their own. They are ahead at half-time, 22–15. The tension grows throughout the second half. The lead slips from five, to three, to nothing. Forty-eight seconds left in the ballgame. If the pipsqueaks from Milan walk off the court right now, the night will still have

From left, Garrett, Jonathan, and Bobby Plump at Plump's Last Shot.

been miraculous. But the pipsqueaks have the ball. Score tied at 30. The players dart. Dribble. Weave. Pass. But nobody shoots. Time out. Eighteen seconds left. The Milan coach draws up a play as his team huddles around him, and 15,000 fans—15,000 fans for a high school basketball game—are standing, cheering. They are witnessing the improbable, they know. If Milan wins, they will have witnessed the impossible.

Milan takes the court. Bobby Plump takes the ball from the referee and tosses it in bounds to Ray Craft. There is confusion. The coach tries to yell above the din of the crowd. Craft tosses it back to Plump. Plump dribbles. Jigs. Jukes. Dodges. Five seconds left. He scrambles. Fake left. Right edge of the free-throw line.

The ball flies.

"When it left my hands," Plump says two generations later without a hint of bragging, "I knew that ball was going in."

So it did. And Bobby Plump, a skinny kid from the plains of southeast Indiana, became the biggest hero in Indiana, perhaps the state's biggest hero of all time, celebrated to this day for "the shot heard 'round the world." The movie *Hoosiers* was based on that shot. The Plump family name is still bounced about on playgrounds, on basketball courts, and in bars all through Indiana. Especially in the bars. Especially in the Indianapolis bar Bobby owns with his son, Jonathan, the bar named, appropriately enough, "Plump's Last Shot."

The original last shot, the one in 1954, changed the Plumps' lives forever. When Jonathan, 36, tells people his last name, invariably they ask if he is related to Bobby. He says, yes, with pride. Bobby, now a successful insurance agent and financial consultant, gives speeches across the state. When Indiana's scholastic sports association moved to make the state's basketball playoffs a "class" system—that is, small schools

would play only small schools, large schools would play only large ones—Bobby Plump appeared before the Indiana legislature, asking it to continue to let kids take a shot at the impossible, like he had.

To understand fully the magnitude of Plump's shot that day, it's necessary to understand what basketball has been to Indiana over the years. The state has produced NBA greats Oscar Robertson, Sean Kemp, and, of course, Larry Bird. Of the fifteen largest high school gymnasiums in the country, fourteen of them are in Indiana, or so the talk goes. High school basketball tournaments have been televised statewide for decades. The day after Milan's victory, the *Indianapolis Star*, the largest paper in the state at the time, devoted three-quarters of its front page to the game.

"For years," explains Bobby, "there weren't any professional teams here. Towns all over this state, what they did was emptied out the streets and filled the gyms. Small towns, especially, it gave them an identity I think." So when Milan, with all of 161 students and only 78 boys, took to the court against Muncie, with close to 2,000 students, there was a natural identification for small towns in every corner of Indiana and every basketball- and corn-fed town in between.

"It was classic David and Goliath," Bobby Plump says. "Everybody in Indiana was pulling for Milan." When the team headed home, after the victory, it was greeted by police cars and fire trucks, lights a-flashing, at the border of nearly every town it drove through. "At one point, we had an eighteen-mile caravan," Plump says. "Cars were parked on the side of the road, the people out cheering us. When we got to Milan, I think they estimated 40,000 people were there for us."

Jonathan Plump listens to his father recount the story for the millionth time. The son, though, shows no signs of boredom, and laughs at every aside his father makes. Jonathan wanted to pay homage to his father—and the son was no fool about capitalizing on the family name. Jonathan had owned a successful restaurant and bar in town, and he knew people would come to a bar devoted to that impossible game on March 20th, 1954. So with his father's blessing (and a chunk of his money), Jonathan opened Plump's Last Shot, which is as much a museum as a restaurant and bar, with memorabilia from Milan hung on every wall and dangling from the ceiling.

"We've had a lot of the high schools coming in, and we're getting more," Jonathan says. "It's a pretty neat thing. These kids come in, they want to meet Dad, they're looking at all these pictures. I've had a lot of opportunities because of Dad. One of the nicest things is people who we don't even know will come up to me and say, 'I remember that game,' 'I'll never forget that.' That kind of stuff. And they're so nice about it.

"It's great he has all this attention for his basketball," continues Jonathan, "but he also happens to be a great dad."

Not surprisingly, Bobby Plump coached his son in basketball from grades four through eight. The father offered pointers, but the most valuable part of that time was spent traveling to tournaments together. They journeyed to Washington, to Missouri, to Canada, and elsewhere. "What I remember most is we had fun but I was treated like anyone else on the team," Jonathan recalls. "Everyone who has never been the coach's son assumes you get special treatment or whatever. If anything, my dad tried to make sure there wasn't any favoritism. He coached to win, and that's how he should have coached. He didn't like to lose."

"Oh, there were some difficult times raising him," concedes Bobby. There were the normal high school experiences chasing girls, drinking beer, not always coming home when he was supposed to, and hiding in silence to avoid talking about his shortcomings. "I felt there had to be some lines of communication always open," Bobby says, "and there's an age where that doesn't always happen. He does have good judgment. Just when he was younger, he didn't always use that judgment wisely. But we got through it. I'd say from a father–son standpoint, it's an excellent relationship. I think it's even a better relationship from a friendship point of view."

While Jonathan clearly savors his relationship with his father, as well as the fame and success his father's shot has brought to the family, basketball has, at times, caused a rift between father and son.

There was the time, for instance, when Jonathan was between his sophomore and junior year in high school. He hurt his knee and playing basketball was difficult, and he sulked about it rather than work harder. "My dad said, 'You know, if I could give you my knee, I would,'" Jonathan recalls. "It was a great thing to say, but I didn't take it very well, and I think that's when I realized my competitiveness wasn't what his was, and I think that hurt him for a while."

But, for the record, Jonathan Plump, while a freshman playing basketball for Cathedral High School against Indianapolis Tech, hit a last-second shot to win the game. The newspaper clipping from that game, at Jonathan's insistence, is not displayed publicly. It hangs in a room off the bar's office. Above the commode.

Jonathan knows, he says, that his shot wasn't as big as his father's, not even close, really. No basketball shot in Indiana history has been as big. Still, Bobby Plump can't help but marvel at just how famous the shot was—and is. They will probably still be talking about it, he figures, when his grandson, Garrett, is old enough to have a drink at the bar.

The Keillors: Garrison and Jason

Garrison Keillor and his son Jason on the set of the "Prairie Home Companion".

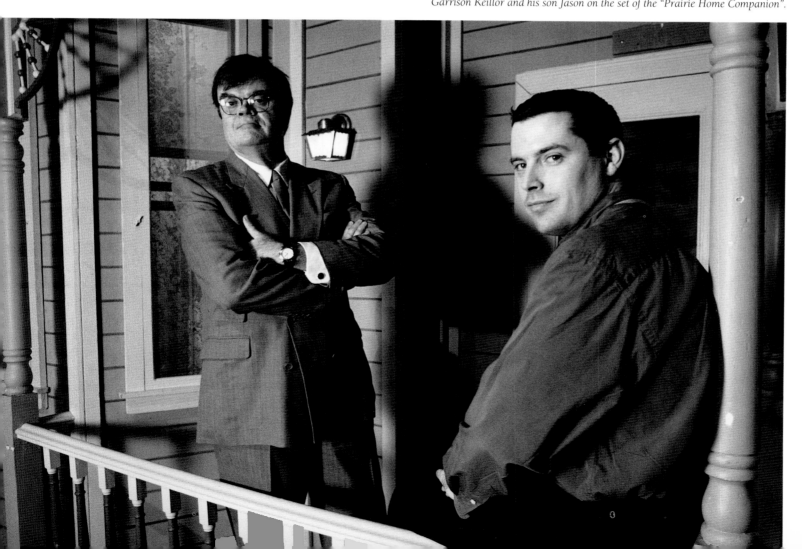

On May 1, 1969, Garrison Keillor's son was born. That fall, Keillor sold his first story to *The New Yorker*, the start of a literary career that would ultimately position him as one of the country's most renowned humorists, a teller of folk stories in the tradition of Mark Twain.

"There was a definite connection between the two events," Keillor, 56, says of the birth of his son, Jason, and the birth of his writing career, which came when he was 26. "The connection was, now I have a child, and now it's time to do with my life what I really want to do with it, and what I really want to do is be a writer. When Jason was on the way, I was working full time, but I sat down evenings and weekends, and I got out the scraps of stories—little pieces of things I'd been toying with for years—and I made them into publishable manuscripts. When I had this child, I became an adult. It was no longer good enough to *want* to be a writer. It no longer did to have vague aspirations. I was going to *be* a writer."

And so he has. With great success. He has written eleven books, including a recent one on Jesse Ventura, the pro wrestler turned Minnesota governor. His radio show, "A Prairie Home Companion," is broadcast on more than 450 public radio stations. His recordings of *Lake Wobegon Days* received a Grammy Award and he has been inducted into the Radio Hall of Fame.

He is sitting on a bench in New York's Central Park, measuring every word he speaks, occasionally closing his eyes as if searching for just the right one, and delivering each with the deep-breathing cadence and sing-song tone that has become as soothing as a sleeping dog on the feet to millions of fans of the radio show he began in 1974. Each Saturday evening, Keillor performs a live variety show like no other. Built around his signature monologue—"The News From Lake Wobegon"—the most familiar place in America that doesn't exist, Keillor captivates some 2.6 million listeners a week. In this mythical Midwest town "where all the children are above average," Keillor spins tales of the locals' trials and tribulations. There are, for instance, the problems Pastor Inkvist is having at Our Lady of Perpetual Indulgence. And there's the man who found himself in trouble while shoveling his roof. He was drinking, took a break, and fell asleep spread-eagled. When he awakened, he found his coat and pants frozen to the shingles, and he was unable to move. Keillor performs the show in front of live audiences in theaters around the country, using sound effects, a small cast, and his own vivid words to paint a mental picture of all variety of people in all variety of situations, most of them—like the spread-eagled man—flat-out silly.

His stage manager: his son, now 30.

"I didn't hire him and I didn't know that it was a good idea for him to work for the show," Keillor says. "I'm all for nepotism. I believe in it, and I believe in fathers offering their sons and daughters an opportunity to get in the family business if one exists and if it's going to be rewarding. But I also think it can be awkward to have your life tied to your father's in that way."

Their relationship on the set is not strained the way some father–son relationships might be when a father and son work together, when too much contact can push them away rather than bring them together. Keillor respects his son for his work, values him as an integral part of the show.

"In a certain respect," Keillor continues after further reflection, "he bosses me around more than I would dare boss him around. One of the reasons he was hired for the job is he could boss me around and other people were hesitant to. But, hey, somebody has to knock on the door and say, 'Five minutes!' You have to be ready to walk on stage and stand in front of that microphone. If your shirt isn't ironed, your shoes aren't tied, it doesn't matter. It's five minutes. You have to be out there."

"But one of my biggest jobs," explains Jason, "is subduing his flights of fancy as far as what is possible to do on a stage. Once, he wanted to do pyrotechnics on stage. He's wanted to fly in on a zipline from the balcony. And usually he comes up with these ideas the day before the show. I'm the one who has to say, 'That's crazy. If you wanted to do that we would need licensed pyrotechnics, permits, all kinds of things that aren't possible to get given the hour.' I think it amuses him to see me put in that position. There are only a couple of people who walk up to him and directly contradict him and what he thinks is possible."

Jason, perhaps, feels comfortable contradicting his father because their relationship is a close one. That hasn't always been the case. When Jason was 5 and 6 years old, Garrison was writing out of the family home in Minnesota while Jason's mother worked at a hospital. Garrison was a stay-home dad in a day when not many existed.

"We lived in St. Anthony Park, a part of St. Paul where you could let your child go out in the morning after breakfast and hook up with the gang of other 5 and 6 year olds, and they could go down to the park and play, and you didn't have to worry about them," he recalls, staring into the clouds as if he's seeing a film of those days. "It was a great place to have a kid. He would come home for lunch, and if he didn't, Mrs. Ferdy would call and ask if he could eat over at her house, and of course it was okay. Then he could wander home at 2 or 3 o'clock, and by that time you've had a great day of writing."

But when Jason was 7, his parents split up. He spent much of his childhood with his mother, seeing his father only on weekends, though more frequently in the summer.

"I was doing the radio show on Saturday, so it was really a cobbled-together relationship," Garrison recalls. "I would go pick him up on Friday, and we'd do something Friday evening, although I was working on the show, and then he'd come to the rehearsal on Saturday."

Since Saturdays were spent with Dad and Dad was doing a radio show, Jason began helping out in any way he could. At first, he sold popcorn in the theater where his father performed. Later, Jason hawked tickets. ("He was quite proud of the day he got to make change at the show," Garrison says.) Although neither father nor son realized it at the time, even as a child Jason was preparing for a career in broadcasting, learning how to manage a show that recalls the old days of radio and has no contemporary parallel. And aside from learning the technical aspects of production, the experience of being around such a broadcast for so many years has given him a confidence to help overcome being "Garrison's son."

"It's difficult because I've always been associated with him," Jason says. "I went on to develop my own production skills, but this job was irresistible. To be working in broadcasting—and on this type of historical broadcast—was too much to pass up. I still wonder sometimes how people think of me doing this job. I meet radio station sponsors, and they realize I'm Garrison's son, and I wonder if they think it's purely some nepotism at work." It's not merely nepotism, though, and Jason knows it. "Really, I can look back and feel like I was being groomed for this job at 7 years old. It's like a natural ritual, like a Sunday dinner."

Garrison says he never intended to groom his son for the job, but thought having him at the show was part of preparing him for life. "I think part of my philosophy was that a child should be included in the adult world as much as possible. A child should be around the parents' work and see what it is and experience it directly," he says. Being at the theater for Jason was interesting, as was experiencing a fictional town like Lake Wobegon, Garrison says, and he believes it had a positive effect on his son.

"People liked having him around and I think it was good for him. He got to know some odd people when he was very small, which I think has made him more tolerant than most people, and I think it's made him very socially skilled. My son is able to deal with all sorts of odd situations, much better than I am. His mother worked with retarded adults, and she made sure he saw a great deal of that, and I think that gave him a great deal of empathy for the underdog, for people who are out of the mainstream. My son, I think, has a profound sense of justice, and he's a very down-to-earth person, but I also think, thanks to his mother, he's not put off by awkward people or by strange behavior. He's a very decent person. I admire that. I don't have that myself; I feign empathy, but I don't feel it as he does."

He does not, though, have to feign empathy when it comes to his son. "You suffer for your children more than you suffered for yourself when you were that age," Garrison says. "I once saw my son play rightfield in a softball game with men, a team I used to play on. He was maybe 12 or 13, a tall, rangy kid, and a very long fly ball was hit to him, and he had to go a few steps to get it. When it bounced off the heel of his glove, I felt pain for my son. He felt bad, I felt a lot worse . . . I just grieved over that pop fly."

Jason's job has had him looking out for his father as well at times. He watches him, corrects him, critiques his shows, and occasionally has to untangle the microphone wires from his wandering boss, who has a penchant for getting tied up in microphone stands. "I've seen all kinds of disasters on the show," Jason says. There was the time, for example, that Garrison was needed from the wings in a hurry because of a mishap involving a guitarist who was performing on the show.

"Sean Blackburn was on," Jason recalls, "and the previous stage manager had failed to mark the edge of the stage. He toppled right over the edge with his 1961 Martin guitar. This is all live on the radio. It created a good twenty seconds of confusion until we could get Garrison to cover for him."

Garrison has no intention of ending his radio show, and certainly not his writing career, and Jason has no plans to leave his father's production any time soon. His mother died in 1998, and his father now has a toddler daughter, Maia Grace, with his wife, Jenny Lind Nilsson. "Probably after all the years and the distance that we've bridged, to now be working together is really great. He has a new family that I love very much, and I feel lucky to have that, especially in the absence of my mother now. If I weren't 30 years old, I'd go and move in again. But it's too late. I'll admire his family from a distance."

Garrison, though, wants to keep his son close. "I come from a religious people who place spiritual truth ahead of family feeling," he says. "In their presence, you often feel like you're not good enough to be around them. So he's my family, really. He's the basis of my family."

And while Garrison isn't out to fire his son, he does think he should consider why he's the stage manager. Is it out of loyalty or because he really enjoys it?

"I think it's a wonderful thing from my point of view. I worry a little bit about him, from his point of view. I wouldn't know how to replace him. Certainly there will come a time when it'll become necessary for him to do something else. I don't think children are supposed to live their lives out of loyalty. I assume he likes the work. At the same time, I think that people probably need to keep moving. Stay loose. I think it's harder to quit a job if you're working for your dad than if you're working for Uncle Sam."

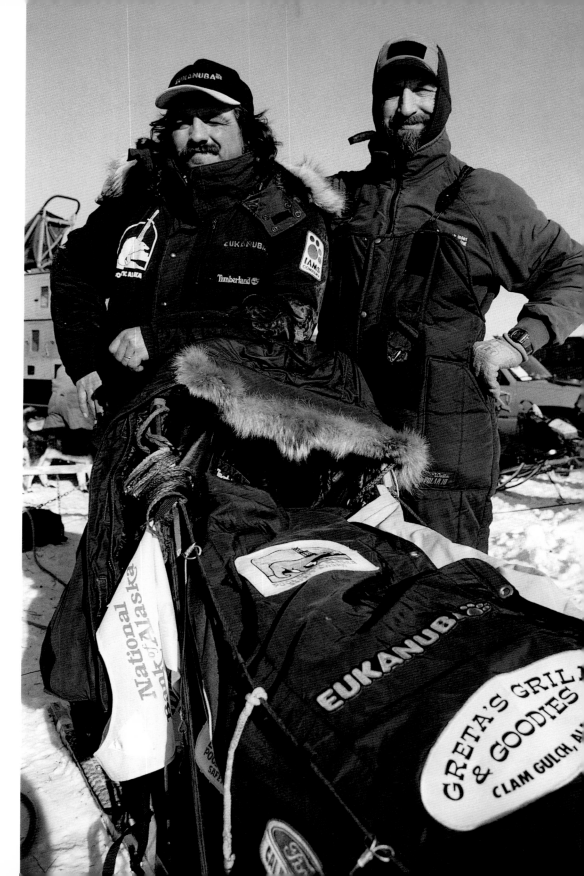

The Osmars: Dean and Tim

From left, Tim and Dean Osmar at the start of the Iditarod.

The prospects for Dean Osmar's survival looked as bad as the weather. He was on Topkok Mountain in the interior of Alaska, just him and his sled and some camping gear and his dogs, as far as he could see, which was not very far at all. Snowflakes whizzed at him like a billion bullets, propelled by winds that whipped at close to seventy miles per hour, just about blinding him.

"I almost died," he says now, wholly without drama, as casually as he might mention that he almost scratched his nose, darn it. "It was a major storm and I got off the trail. It was such a struggle; it was sort of a nightmare. What happened was, I wore myself to complete exhaustion."

Dean left the dogs—"something you should never do," he says—struggled back to the trail on foot, then trudged back to find his team. He tipped his sled on its side for cover, then climbed into a sleeping bag until the storm abated and he could continue. "It was," he says, "a little uncomfortable."

Such are the travails for competitors in what is arguably the world's toughest competition, the Iditarod. "The Last Great Race On Earth," as it is known, is a 1,000-mile-plus dogsled race through the uninhabited interior of Alaska, from Anchorage to Nome. Temperatures often drop to sixty degrees below zero, as the competitors race through windswept wilderness on trails that alternate between sea ice and the frozen tundra. Storms come suddenly and violently. The one that nearly killed Dean swept in during his first try at the race, in 1982, but it wasn't enough to deter him from running again.

In 1984, he won it.

"And that was it for me," he explains. "I said, I won it, I got it out of my system, that's it, I'm finished."

But when Dean, 52, hung up the snowshoes, his son Tim, 31, began putting down some tracks of his own on the trail. A winner of the junior version of the competition, he has been racing in the Iditarod since 1985, finishing as high as third but still sledding for that first victory.

"The thing is, I'd like to win the darn thing, and there's no way to win if you don't run it," he says. "So I have to run." If he does win, the Osmars would be the first father and son to do it since Rick and Dick Mackey won in 1978 and 1983, respectively.

Dean's experience with the race and Tim's current quest have worked to bring an already close father and son even closer. Dean took up the race at the relatively ancient age of 32, and he and his son, not yet a teenager, would train together. "When we first started, Tim was 12 and I was twenty years older, but it was like we were growing up together," Dean recalls. "We built fires. It was thirty below, and we'd camp out and sit around telling lies. We both loved the camping so much. We did it for years and years until he left the nest."

The danger involved in racing the Iditarod, too, has worked in their favor. It has pushed the father and son to appreciate what they have and reminded them not to take anything for granted. They are no strangers to harsh conditions, though. Life as commercial fishermen in the Osmars' south central Alaskan town of Clam Gulch can be perilous. They're up early, to bed late, on rough seas during most of their working hours, and all the while their economic livelihood is as uncertain as what lurks in the water below them. Tim began captaining one of his father's skiffs at age 14. It was—and is—tough, often brutal work, a type of fishing that takes place within a mile or so of shore, where the rough tidal currents, innumerable rocks, and countless sandbars all invite disaster.

"We set nets, and every five hours we'd go out and take the salmon from the nets," says Dean. "This is four times a day, sometimes for a two-week period straight. You go out for three hours, get an hour nap, mend nets, grab a bite to eat, head back out. You might work twelve hours on the water and three or four hours on land, and with the rest of the time you try to eat something and get some sleep. It can be dangerous enough, but then you add the fatigue. . ."

"There was one day, maybe in 1980," Tim recalls, "when we set the net and there was this huge, unexpected big run of fish come in. Boom! We had 2,000 fish in our net. We were so underhanded, my mom was in my bow, and it was just me and her and we had to fill the boat up with 700 fish or so. You get the boat pointed the wrong way like that—or you get too many fish in it and get it turns sideways. Being older and wiser now, I try not to get in those situations. But it can be a little bit hair-raising for sure at times."

"We've been lucky not to lose any crew," adds Dean, whose company now owns ten fishing boats. Tim owns two of his own. "It doesn't sound like much, but believe me, you get too many fish in your boat and you can be in real trouble. You'll be fishing all week, get twenty or thirty fish a day, then all of a sudden there's 1,500 fish, and you're trying to get every one. The boats start to take on water, and it gets pretty scary. We've had several times when we had to send out rescue crews."

For the Osmars, though, the end of the fishing season doesn't mean it's time to sit back and relax. Rather, for years now the end of their time on the water has meant the beginning of more intense training on land for the Iditarod. And, year round, both Dean and Tim breed and raise sled dogs. When the dogs are old enough, they're hooked up to four-wheelers on the Alaskan beaches. They train every other day usually beginning sometime in August, running four to six miles, building their way up until October, when they begin to train with sleds.

"They have a purpose in life—their own purpose," says Dean. "All they want to do is run."

Dean had long been interested in dog mushing but could never afford the dogs. Not until 1979. That's when he traded an old skiff for three puppies—Red, Boots, and Prince—who would eventually become the leaders of his Iditarod-winning sled.

The father and son have never competed against each other in the big race, but they have run in the same lesser events. In 1984, the year Dean won the Iditarod, for example, they went up against each other in the Tustumena 200. Tim won it.

"He wanted to win, but if it was going to be someone else, I'm sure he was glad it was me," Tim says. "We met up at a checkpoint fifty miles from the end of race. I pulled in there. It was crowded and hot, so I said I was going to go to another cabin about a mile down the trail. Well, I just kept going and got about an hour lead on them. In dog racing, it's not always the fastest team. Sometimes it's strategy and luck that wins it for you."

That strategy and luck has eluded Tim in the Iditarod, but he intends to keep at it. He was in a network television helicopter when his father was racing to victory in 1984, and that's when he decided he had to give it a try. "I don't know if you'd call it electrifying, but it was something like that," Tim says. "I got the fever then and figured I could do it too. I haven't pulled it off yet, but who knows?"

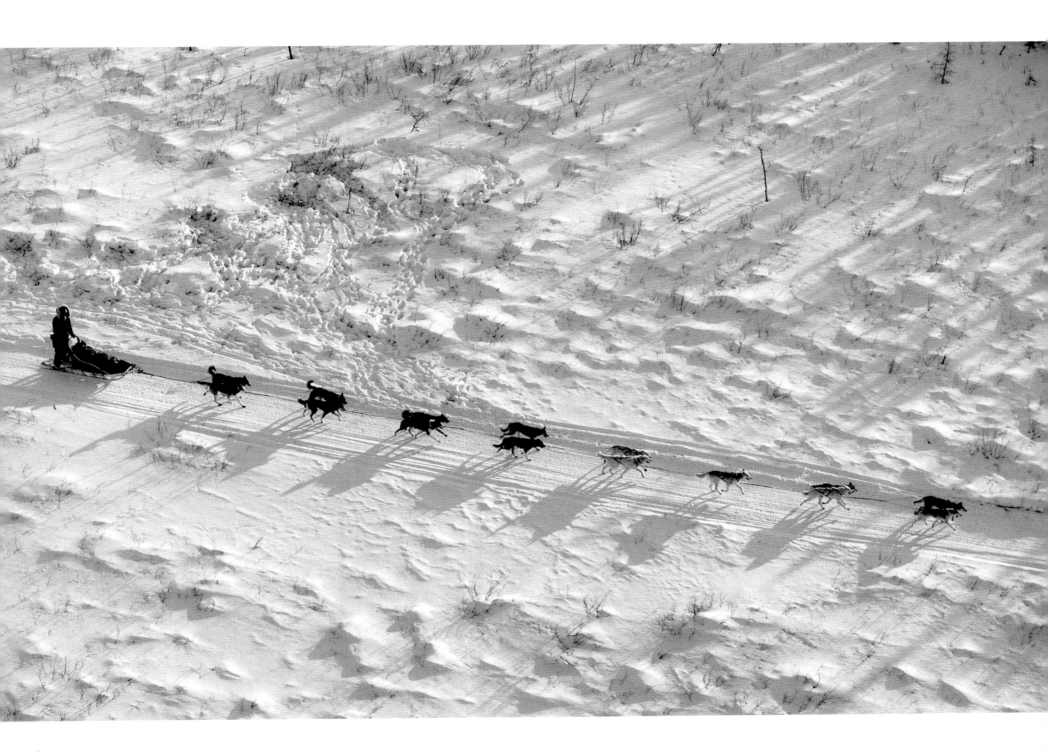

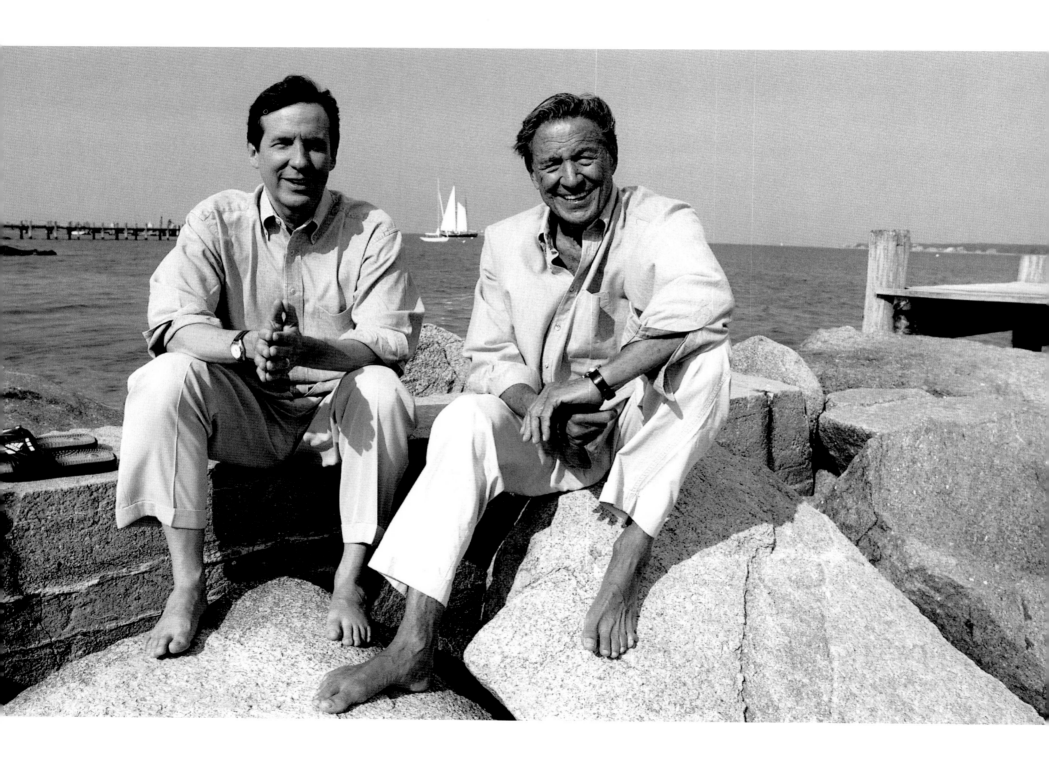

The Wallaces: Mike and Chris

M ike Wallace remembers it vividly. Of course he would: It was 1962 and his son Peter, 19, was living in France. "All of a sudden, we didn't hear from him and didn't hear from him, and I got on an airplane to find him," Wallace recalls, finding it uncomfortable—unlike when *he's* doing the interviewing—to maintain eye contact with his visitor. He found the youth hostel where Peter was staying, and his belongings were still there. Some people at the hostel said Peter wanted to climb a mountain near the Gulf of Corinth to get a better look at a monastery where two nuns were living. So, Wallace, accompanied by a guide, rode a donkey to the top of the cliff.

"We sat down to catch our breath, and we're sitting there like this," Wallace remembers, hunched over, forearms on his knees. "I looked down, and about 150 feet down we saw somebody—and there he was."

Wallace's elder son lay dead from a fall. As Wallace says, now gently punching a fist into the side of his left thigh, searching for the sentiment: "It was a pain

Chris Wallace and his father Mike relax on Martha's Vineyard.

you really can't put into words. There's no real feeling quite like losing a child, especially this young man. He was in the first full flush of really finding himself."

For Mike Wallace, his son's death would not come without new life—on two fronts. Peter's fall from the cliff marked the beginning of a journalism career unrivaled in broadcast history. For nearly forty years, Wallace has been one of the most respected—and most feared—interviewers in all of television journalism, a three-decades-plus veteran of *60 Minutes* with a knack for penetrating the armor of everyone from the Ayatollah Khomeini to Malcolm X. An unblinking interviewer, he has sparred with presidents and thugs and has gotten the better of most of them. He made Barbra Streisand cry.

But more than a storied journalism career, Peter's death also marked the rebirth of Mike's relationship with younger son Chris. Now a respected broadcast figure in his own right, Chris has served as chief White House correspondent for NBC News and co-anchor of the network's *Today* show; at ABC News he is currently chief correspondent for *20/20* and a regular fill-in host for Ted Koppel's *Nightline*.

Paradoxically, Peter's death, while helping forge a new relationship between Mike and Chris, also created a barrier between the two survivors.

The Wallaces are sitting on the screened back patio of the father's home on Martha's Vineyard, and with nearly every story they share one of them fills in the details for the other or corrects him or tosses in a remark such as, "I never knew that," and the other assures him that, yes, it certainly is true.

This is a father and son, one in his eighties the other in his fifties, who are still learning about each other, making up for years and years lost to a variety of circumstances: a divorce before Peter's death, the presence of an influential stepfather for Chris, and, perhaps more than anything else, that hall-of-fame career that seems to make Mike Wallace tick more than the pacemaker planted in his chest.

"We certainly have had our voyage of discovery to get where we are today," says Chris, now thoroughly enjoying his relationship with his father. "After my parents were divorced, I was living in Chicago, and he was in New York, and going to visit him . . . it was more of an obligation than any kind of pleasure. It was like seeing a distant uncle rather than this man who was supposed to be my father."

In fact, for many years, Chris called his stepfather, Bill Leonard, "Dad." His biological father he called—and still does—"Mike".

But with Peter's death came a question for both Mike and Chris, at least at the subconscious level: How many regrets are out there floating in the houses of the living and buried in the graves of the dead? The accident sparked an epiphany for both of them.

"Peter's death, it created a big change between my father and me," Chris says. "There was much more of a sense in this relationship that you just couldn't take it for granted and pick it up whenever. I think there was a real sea change after we lost Peter. It does make you take stock of your family, of the impermanence of life, and of what's important."

There was no formal pronouncement from either father or son, no, "From now on, we will love each other and act accordingly." There was simply a decided effort to spend more time together, and it's through time and shared memories and common experiences and discoveries that father–son bonds are forged.

"You begin to have experiences that make for a relationship," Chris says. "There was this one Christmas, and Mike had done some work

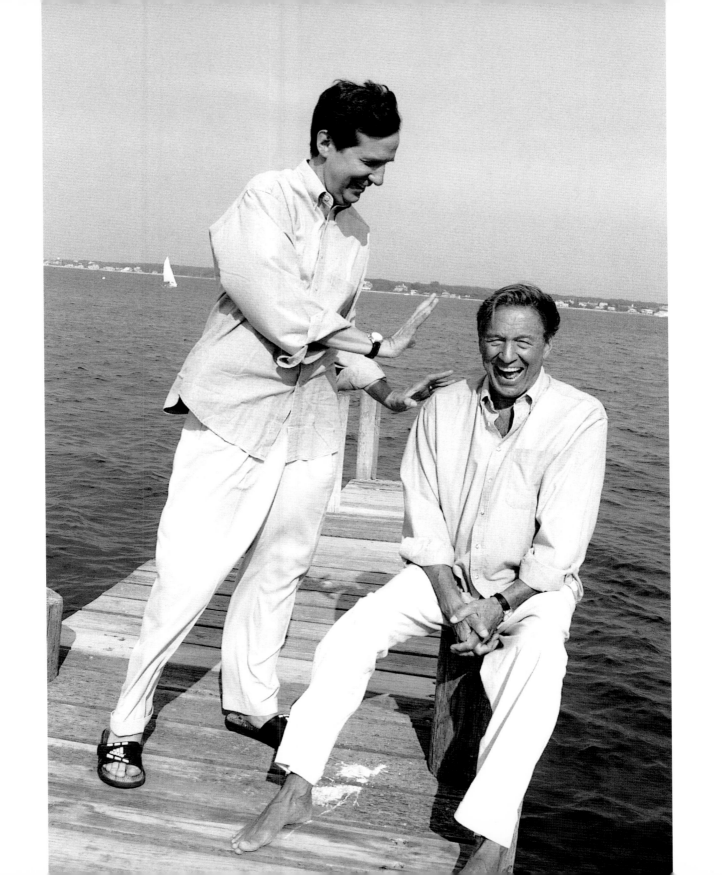

for Zenith. There was this record player with two speakers that he had given me—"

"—I'll never forget this," Mike interrupts with a laugh—one of those shared memories.

Chris needed to catch a train to return to school, one he thought was leaving from Grand Central Station. It wasn't. When he and his father realized that, they went into a mad sprint to get where they were supposed to be.

"I grabbed my suitcase," Chris continues, "and Mike grabs that stereo, and we're running down the street, and I thought Mike was about to have a heart attack—"

"—What I did was get a hernia," his father interrupts again. "I really did."

"It's a stupid story," says Chris. "But it's the kind of event that makes you a father and son to each other, at least for a few minutes. It's not just through one event like that that you build this relationship; it's hundreds of little things like that. We started spending more time together and we started building all of these little things like that and we got to where we are now."

"As far as I'm concerned," his father says in a deadpan, "that particular event broke up the relationship for a long time."

But while Peter's death pushed Mike and Chris into situations like running through the streets of New York together with a stereo in their arms, Mike's career often served to keep them apart. And that career, too, was a result of Peter's death. For years, Mike Wallace had wanted to be a serious journalist. With divorces and remarriages, though, he had four children to help support.

But, after Peter's death that "impermanence of life" that Chris talks about also struck his father in a professional sense. Mike Wallace had been making commercials, introducing *The Lone Ranger* on radio broadcasts, and doing "rip-and-read" news shows, but nothing like serious investigative reporting. Peter's goal was to be a professional newsman, and with his death came a mission for his father.

"All those years I dismissed it, saying 'I have all of these kids to support,'" recalls Mike. "With Peter's death, that made me say to heck with everything else. I took off a year, and I was going to do nothing but look for a job in news. I had always wanted to, but news just didn't pay sufficiently, really, and I could make a fair amount of money doing other things."

In about seven months, he convinced CBS to give him a job in its news division, and by 1968 he was one of the network's two correspondents, along with Harry Reasoner. His coverage of the turbulent 1968 presidential election helped Mike land a job on *60 Minutes*. It also convinced Chris, who was on hand as a gopher, that he wanted to get into journalism. "It was great," he remembers. "It was as if I couldn't believe people were getting paid to do this. I thought it was the most fun you could have without being arrested."

With his career in full flight, Mike, according to his son, had little time for him and his sister, Pauline. For his part, Mike maintains he was striking a balance between career and family, and it is during this type of conversation that the old tensions in their relationship become evident—just as its obvious strength helps them overcome these disagreements.

Chris has managed to stay close to his children despite a demanding and successful career of his own. (He has interviewed everyone from Bill Clinton to Michael Jordan and has exposed such stories as problems with the B-2 Stealth bomber and wealthy American expatriates who gave up their citizenship to avoid paying U.S. taxes.)

Part of that, he says, was learned from his stepfather, who—unlike Mike—saw nothing wrong with his children accompanying him at work.

"I think, frankly, it has a lot less to do with the balance than with the individual involved," Chris says. "Mike adores me and adores my sister, but what he really *loves* is his work. I think it's possible to have both the career and pay more attention to the family."

"For me," adds Chris, a father of two children from his first marriage and four that came with his second, "I think I've always been more interested in truly balancing the two. I think I've had a much closer relationship with my kids than my father had with his."

"No," disagrees Mike, using his close relationship with his daughter as an example. "If I may . . . it's not true. My relationship with Pauline has been like that. You may not realize that, but it's true. Look, there are a lot of things that get in the way of a close relationship between a father and a son—or a father and a daughter for that matter. Some things got in the way of our relationship, but I still think I was striving for a balance."

And there are things that bring a relationship back together. While Mike and Chris made their move toward a strong relationship after Peter's death, it wasn't until well into adulthood, when Chris was going through a divorce of his own, that the relationship became bulletproof.

"I always felt there was a certain brittleness—there was a bit of scar tissue that hadn't been overcome," Chris says. "In 1990 or so, I went through this very disorienting period when I was getting divorced. For two months—no matter where I was in the world and where my father was—he called me and we talked. It could have been a two-minute conversation and just, 'Hey, how are you?' or it

could have been a twenty-minute conversation where we got into things, but he called every day. That was the point where I think any scar tissue, any resentment, for me went away."

And now, sitting on Martha's Vineyard, chiding each other, correcting each other, laughing with each other, and still learning about each other, Mike and Chris are at peace with their relationship. The death of a son and a brother, the father's divorce and the son's own breakup, the time spent apart—painful as it all was—served a purpose because both worked through it.

"There were times he was a disinterested father—and as I reflect on this, there were times I was a disinterested son," Chris says. "Through all of that, one of us could have gotten tired of it all and just given up, but we didn't, and that's made all the difference in both of our lives."

Mike agrees. Talking about the past is clearly painful at times, but he looks at a column of his life's pluses and minuses and he is satisfied. He has been married to his current wife, Mary, since 1986. He is surrounded by grandchildren. He is talking to Chris—really talking. Losing a child was painful, of course, and can never be minimized; but gaining one has been pure bliss.

"The fact that I have him and my grandchildren and my daughter and her children and Mary and her kids—I can't tell you how satisfying that is," Mike says. "It took a long time. There's a picture in there," he says, pointing toward his dining room. "It was taken on my eightieth birthday, and there's a family in that picture, and in this house there's a family, and the fact that we have this—we really *do* have this—that's what's finally nice for me.

"And," he adds—no problem with eye contact now—"I'm still working."

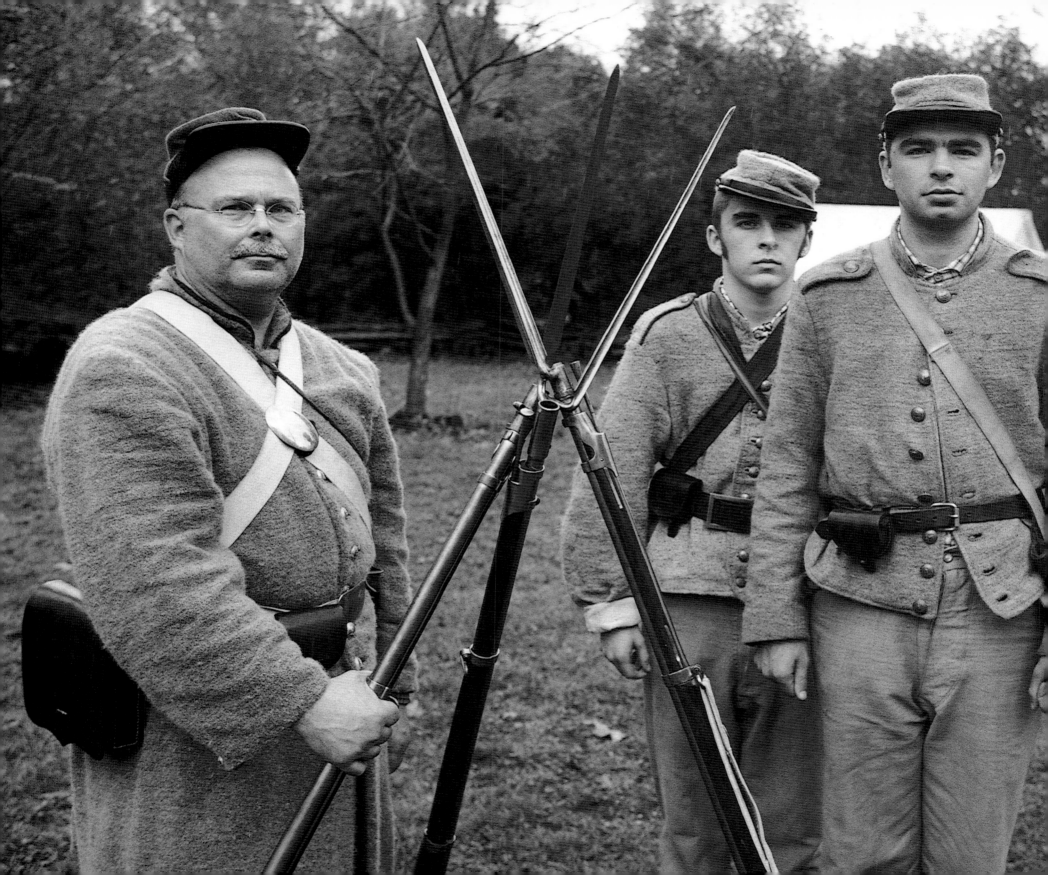

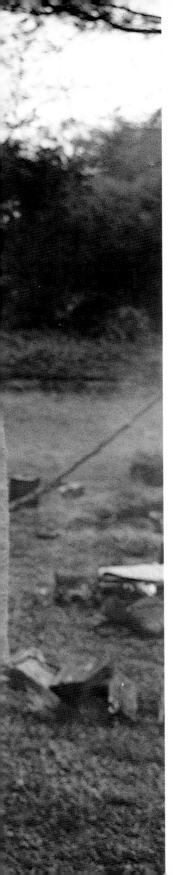

The Pokorskis: Paul, Victor, and Stephen

The temperature is dropping, to right about freezing, and the rain is falling hard. The January night is a good one for staying inside, comfortable on a couch with a warm drink and a favorite blanket.

But for Paul Pokorski and his sons, Victor and Stephen, a couch is out of the question. In fact, the indoors is out of the question. And you know what? Raincoats are out of the question, too, the weather be damned. These Pokorski guys are hardcore, and they are going camping. They will have no waterproof clothing, no high-tech tents, no sleeping bags to keep those cold temperatures from making them shake in their tall black boots. They will camp, and they will do it just as Civil War soldiers did, right down to their damp, scratchy woolen underwear.

"I like to experience life the way they did," explains Paul, who in real life is a Virginia Beach firefighter. "They did it with no modern conveniences. What I like is, I'll come across an obstacle and say 'okay, those soldiers must have run into this. What did they do?'"

From left, Paul, Stephen, and Victor Pokorski prepare for battle in Virginia Beach.

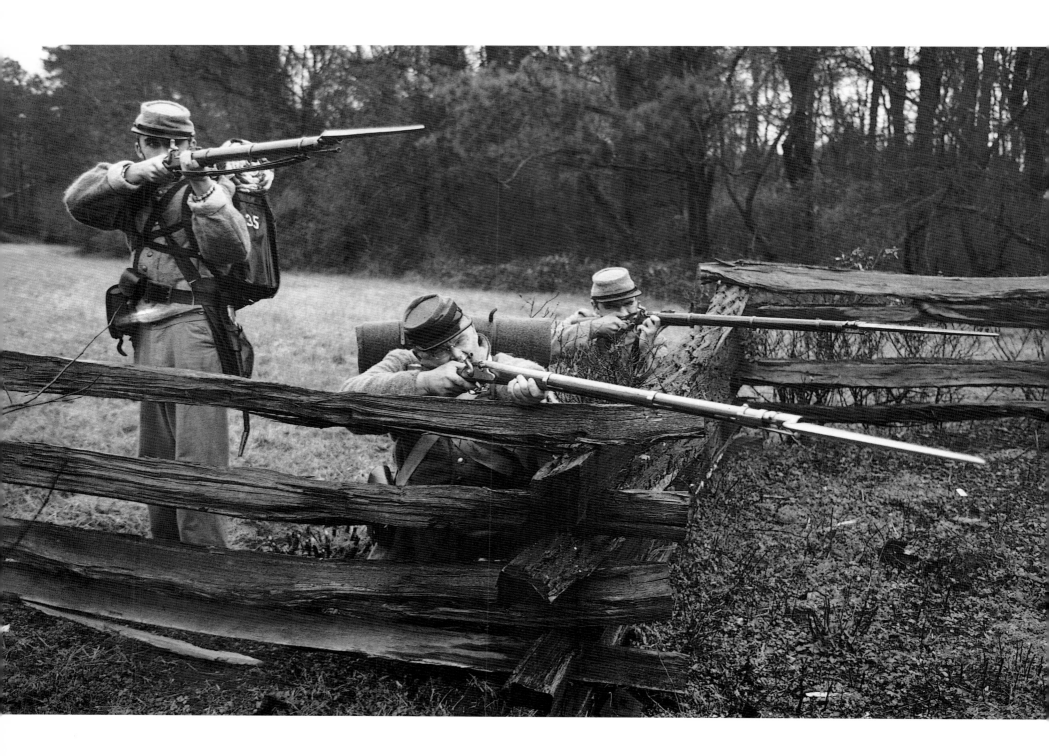

The Pokorskis are part of a growing breed of Civil War reenactors who go far beyond merely wearing the uniforms of the era and instead take extreme measures to adopt the brutal life style of the Civil War soldiers, living the history rather than chatting about it. Across the country, and especially near the former battlefields of the Confederacy, there are men like the Pokorskis who spend their weekends mimicking the soldiers right down to the food they ate and the conditions they faced while in the field—whether it be ninety-five-degree heat with glue-like humidity or freezing cold, with raindrops splashing on their faces.

So, on this night they are dressed in Confederate gray. They wear wool uniforms that scratch like sandpaper, the father peeking through wire-rimmed glasses with dime-sized lenses. They will not order pizza or cook hamburgers over a propane grill. They will cook fatback on a split canteen over a fire.

To stay warm on this night in Virginia Beach, the "soldiers" use body heat from each other by "spooning." They snuggle, eight or more men in a row, all in the fetal position, chests to backs, front thighs to back thighs, arms draped across each other.

"You'd be surprised," Paul says, "how warm that can be."

Theories abound about why so many people are attracted to the life of the reenactor and why some take it to such extremes. Some people believe the reenactors are reincarnated soldiers; some of the reenactors are fascinated by the military; reenactors themselves say that a tiny percentage of their comrades are still fighting the war. But a more accurate clue may be found in the Pokorskis, who like it not only because they want to honor fallen soldiers, but because it has bolstered their relationships with each other.

"It brought out a different side of my dad that I didn't see much,"

explains Victor, 18. "We started seeing his more adventurous side, the more creative side of him. He's usually big on cooking at the campsites, and he reads all these books, and any time we have a conversation he'll bring something up. When we're at the campsites he'll say something like, 'Did you know they did this or that?' and it's always something we didn't know."

Adds Stephen, 16: "It gives us a chance to be with him. He used to have so many meetings and fire department things, we didn't get to see him much. Now he's into something that all three of us can do together and get into. It's also a lot of fun. All of a sudden we just found this, and it clicked. A lot of what I've learned about the Civil War I've learned from him."

Paul enthuses, "Really, I feel a sense of pride to see them on their own when we reenact. They can fend for themselves when it comes time to cooking around the fire and when we go into battle scenarios. They go through the motions with the same vigor that you think a soldier would have."

For the Pokorskis, genealogy and a love for history also play into their attraction for the lifestyle. The father is only too glad to share that with his sons, to pass down the traditions of the South and lessons from that bloodiest of American wars, always instilling in them the importance of honoring the fallen soldiers.

"I'm really pleased beyond words that they want to be there and be with me doing this," Paul says. "We just have a good time being together, I guess. The important thing is, we do this for a sense of remembrance and respect for the soldiers, both North and South, who died during the war. Sometimes we get looked at funny because we're the Confederates and some people see us as the bad guys or they figure we're trying to remember slavery or something. That troubles us because that's not the reason we wear the gray or carry the battle flag. It's in remembrance of the men who actually fought, living for five long years the way they had to live."

Despite the opportunity for bonding with their father, Stephen and Victor weren't immediately overwhelmed by the prospect of reenacting. It grew on them. Some of their friends, at first, questioned why they'd want to spend their weekends in uncomfortable uniforms under such conditions. "But they get really interested once I explain it to them," Victor says. "I don't know that all of them get to spend so much time with their fathers."

Paul has not been able to trace direct forefathers who fought in the Civil War. But he has a feeling one is out there. He points out that his wife's great-grandfather was a corporal in the Army of Northern Virginia, detailed as a regimental musician. Her grandfather played cello, and she plays clarinet. And their son Stephen—long before he had information about his Civil War ancestor—toured with the drum corp.

"There's a direct musical lineage from Civil War soldier to high school student today," Paul says. "Goosebumps kind of jumped on me when I found out about the connections. So I'm thinking maybe the pull I have toward this is due to something in my ancestral heritage that I've yet to find. Maybe it's just the connection through my wife, I don't know, but there's something that makes me want to keep doing it, through the adversity of the weather and walking everywhere and the exhaustion, so I figure it must be something subliminal down deep, something spiritual of a sort, which probably comes from a relative."

Stephen agrees: "When I found out about my great-great grandfather—when I think about going out and portraying him—I want to portray it the way he would have done it. I don't want to go out there and portray it like it was easy. I don't want to lie about it."

None of them deny the hobby appears odd to others—including other reenactors who are dedicated more to comfort than to authenticity. There is a growing split—and even a growing bitterness—between reenactors like the Pokorskis and the others. People like the Pokorskis are referred to by some within the hobby as "hardcores" or "authentics." But they are "stitch counters" to those who deride them for what they see as a neurotic attention to detail. Those who dislike them most, call them "button pissers," for a technique some use to make their buttons tarnish into a more authentic look—by urinating on them.

Whatever, the hardcores say. They are authentic. They prefer "encampments" to battle reenactments. Without live ammunition and blood, they reason, battles are not authentic (though even many hardcores are drawn to battle and will make exceptions). They set up campsites that are wholly devoid of anything—anything—that the soldiers did not have during the war. They eat fatback or gristle. They sleep without tents. They will not use bug spray (they rub onions on their skin), or frying pans (they use the split canteen), or real toothpaste (they use baking soda), or toilet paper (the alternative to which will not be discussed here). They refer to people who are not as authentic as they are as Farbs, either for "Far be it for me" or "Far from authentic." They can give the insults as well as they can receive them.

That's not a battle, though, that Paul wants any part of.

"It shouldn't be a bitterness," he says. "It was a war. It was brutal, but of course it made a better country for us. I just want people—when they see the reenactors—I don't want them to think of us as a bunch of crazy cowboys with nothing better to do. I want them to look at us and recognize that we do it to honor the men who fought for so long."

The Farrell-Forsteins: Carrie, Marshall, Scott, Randy, and George

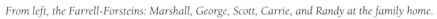

From left, the Farrell-Forsteins: Marshall, George, Scott, Carrie, and Randy at the family home.

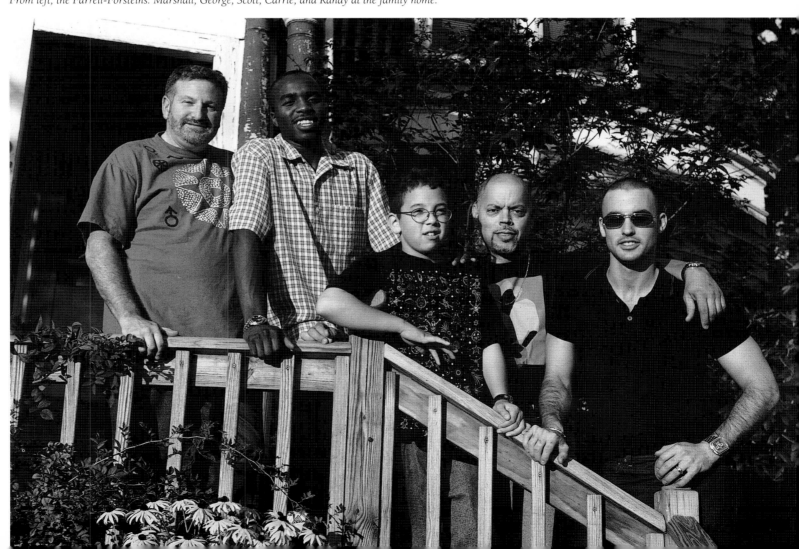

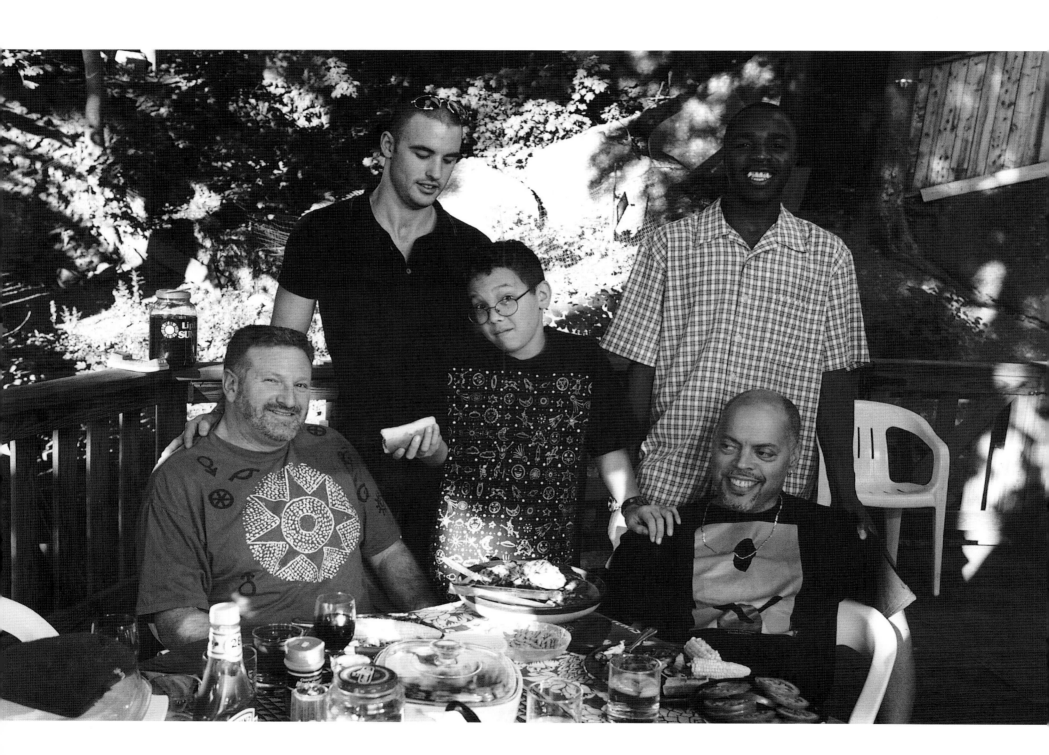

They were a young couple, established in their community, successful professionals, bright futures ahead of them, and deeply, deeply in love. They were, in most every way, perfect candidates for adopting a child, which is precisely what they wanted to do. But the couple, Carrie Farrell and Marshall Forstein, were not perfect candidates in the eyes of Massachusetts. The state decided the infant they wanted to care for, the one whose mother was dead and father had split, would be better off shuttled between foster homes than living with this couple. The reason: Carrie Farrell and Marshall Forstein are gay. It also didn't help that one was black, the other white.

For two very "out" gay men accustomed to questioning the establishment, being a gay bi-racial couple was not a good enough reason to forego adopting a child. They would fight.

Farrell and Forstein met on October 23, 1980, at a party in San Francisco. Their story as a couple is remarkable only in how typical it has been. At the party, they gravitated to each other. "I remember he seemed a little eccentric, which I liked," Farrell says. "And he seemed like he was enjoying himself, which I also liked. And best of all, he didn't look like he was blitzed. I went over and talked to him and we went into a bedroom, closed the door, sat on the floor, and talked for two or three hours straight." Adds Forstein: "The topic of wanting kids came up that very first night."

Like many young couples, they soon faced difficult decisions about their future together. In this case, Massachusetts General Hospital offered Forstein a residency that young doctors only dream about. Would they split up? What about that desire for family? "I was ready to move," Farrell says. "We would go together."

So, on Memorial Day weekend, 1981, with $400 between them, they set out in a ten-year-old Volvo stationwagon that soon had no reverse, no third-gear, and very little in the way of willpower. They got a flat tire in Salt Lake City—with everything they owned packed atop the spare. They had to sneak their dog, Bacchus, into the cheap hotels they stayed in. They hit one of the Midwest's infamous summer thunderstorms and, finally, arrived in Reston, Virginia, at the home of Forstein's parents—at midnight. The next day, they were on their way to Boston. "It was," Forstein says in typical understatement, "an ordeal."

They joke about the ad they placed: "Inter-racial gay couple with large dog needs two-bedroom place with yard in heart of Boston—for under $600."

By 1984, with Farrell working as a social worker and Forstein finishing his residency, talk about having a child turned serious. They bought a house in the Jamaica Plain section of Boston, with raising a child in mind. "We were the first couple in New England to go to an agency and say, 'We're gay and we want to adopt a child,'" Forstein recalls. The reaction at the agency was not initially favorable. They were "studied" at home for nine months. By all accounts they were able to offer a stable, caring home.

"And then this woman says to us, 'I really like you guys, I think you'd make good parents, but politically we just can't handle this right now'," Farrell says. "We were heartbroken. We were just about to throw up our hands we were so discouraged." Then they learned of Ilien Adoptions International of Atlanta, Georgia. A Mexican-American infant named Scott was there. His mother had died shortly after his birth. Nobody knew where his father was. The boy was with the Department of Social Services.

Farrell and Forstein rushed down to Atlanta and interviewed with Ilien. They took Scott, 2½ months old, to the mall. They returned the little boy to Social Services. They waited five days in a motel suite to learn whether they would be allowed to adopt him. For two weeks they got no answer.

"Then we got a call," says Forstein, "and the woman said, 'Come on down and pick him up.'"

"And then," adds Farrell, "our lives changed forever."

The *Oprah Winfrey Show* and other television shows contacted the new family, wanting to tell their story. Farrell and Forstein flatly rejected all offers. They wanted to raise their son not as a first or as a freak but as any other couple would raise their son. "That was very important to us," declares Forstein. "We wanted nothing more than to be treated as a normal family, and the best way we knew to do that was to act like a normal family."

In 1991, Farrell and Forstein asked Scott if he would mind having a brother. A gay young man they knew, Randy, was ostracized from his family, and in need of a place to stay. "I told them, 'You gave me a home when I needed one,'" says Scott, a sixth-grader now. "People may think this isn't normal or whatever, but what's normal? Some family where the parents are always fighting or they don't take care of their kids? One time this boy came up to me and said, 'Ah, you have a gay father!' And I said, 'I have two gay fathers.'"

Says Randy, now in his twenties: "They always said they wanted another child, just without the diapers." So he became their foster child. Two years after joining the family, he had his name legally changed to Randy Britten Farrell-Forstein. "I just felt after all they did for me, the relationship that we've had, that it was something I wanted to do." The fathers have since reached out to another youth, George, offering him a home as well. Those arrangements are still being worked out.

There are a few rules at the Farrell-Forstein house: The parents want to know where their kids are; Friday and Saturday meals are to be eaten as a family; Sunday brunch, be there. Normal enough. But there is no escaping that this family is far from traditional. Farrell is bi-racial; Forstein is white and Jewish; Scott is Mexican; Randy is white; George, who may someday become the newest formal member of the family, is black. The parents say, though, that the neighborhood has welcomed them. When Scott came home with them for the first time, in fact, the neighbors threw a party. And most any parent would wish for a 12-year-old boy as seemingly well-adjusted as Scott, who is precocious and smart.

"Oh, there's some teasing," he admits. "I just think, well, I have a lot of friends. I live in a good community with a lot of safe places and a lot of educational places. So my parents are gay and I'm going to complain? People used to hurt my feelings by saying a lot of mean stuff, about living with a lot of gay people around me. I either just walk away or I look at them and say, 'Hey, get a life. Get over it.'"

"He's just always assumed," says Forstein, "that people who had problems with us being gay—that it was their problem. What we have in this house is a family."

Farrell and Forstein wrestled with whether to make their story public, to appear in a book with Randy, George, and Scott. Although they turned down the earlier television offers, they felt that Scott was now old enough to decide whether he wanted the family's story told. He did, and so did Randy.

"I'd like to be on *Oprah*, too," Scott says. "People could see that we're not freaks or anything."

"We've always faced the question," explains Forstein, "of how do we stand up and be counted on to make our statement and still protect our privacy? On the one hand, we don't find anything particularly extraordinary about our family. On the other hand, we want other people to see what is possible."

The Mannings: Archie, Cooper, Peyton, and Eli

Archie Manning and his sons, from left, Peyton, Cooper, and Eli kick back in New Orleans.

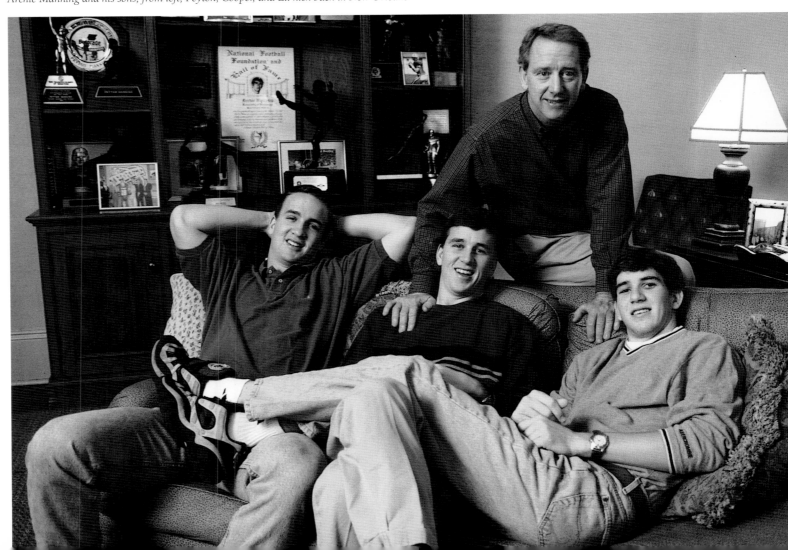

When it comes to his three sons, Archie Manning, the great 1970s and 1980s NFL quarterback, has much to be proud of: Cooper, once a promising football player, has overcome a potentially devastating medical problem to become a successful businessman and sports personality. Peyton, the former University of Tennessee star, is now a successful NFL quarterback with a $48-million contract with the Indianapolis Colts. And Eli, another football prodigy considered last year by some to be one of the nation's top quarterback prospects, just landed at his parents' alma mater, Ole Miss.

But when Archie Manning talks about his sons, their accomplishments on the football field and in the business world barely come up. He is proud of them not because they make a lot of money or throw touchdown passes, but because of how they get along with him and especially because of how they get along with each other. Because, in his words, they're "good guys." Corny? To be certain. True? Absolutely.

"I hit my knees and count my blessings all the time," Manning says in his Garden District home in New Orleans. "I tell them if they really, really want to disappoint me, just don't get along when they're adults. The fact that they do get along and are very close, very good friends, is as satisfying to me as anything." Agrees Peyton, from the family living room: "We are friends. All the football accomplishments, they're all well documented. But what's been most important to me—the best times in my life—they've been right in there, in that kitchen, over meals. What's really more important than that?"

Of course, for some, this is the family that is too All-American, too perfect. The father and sons have handled themselves so well over the years, in fact, that they have actually been knocked for it. Must be an act, people say. No father is that good. No sons, either. Peyton

Manning's classy response when he finished second in the 1997 Heisman Trophy voting? Must have been phony. His refusal to pass up an autograph seeker? Must be public relations spin.

Then you listen to them talk, listen to their values, their upbringing, the way they interact with each other, speak of each other, and you realize: In these days of spoiled sports stars stuck on self-importance, the Mannings are real people. They don't act the way they think they're expected to, but simply the way they are—an extremely close, exceptionally gracious family who have avoided the pitfalls of fame.

Archie Manning has been the example, although he had no real example of his own, not since he first entered adulthood, anyway. Archie's father took his own life when Archie was 19, already a football star at Ole Miss. "When something like that happens, I think you grow up real fast," Manning says. "I think I was fairly mature, but nobody had really thrown any real responsibility on me. All of a sudden, I had my mother to worry about, my family. I had about two weeks before football practice started. I told my mother I'd do what-ever it took, I'd quit school if I had to. But we managed. You know, I don't think it hit me till three or four weeks later. I was back at school, and it just hit me that he wasn't going to be around, that he wasn't going to be at any of my games, that my mother wasn't going to have a husband, that my sister wasn't going to have a father. I don't think I cried till later. Then I had some emotional moments."

Peyton recalls: "When we got to be about his age—the age when he lost his father, I mean—I really sensed him getting closer to us. He'd buddy-up to us more, put his arm around our necks and hug us to him, that sort of thing. I really think losing his father at that age had a lot to do with that."

Archie Manning, of course, did not quit school. He eventually graduated from Ole Miss a consensus pick as the best college quarterback in the country and went on to become one of the NFL's premier quarterbacks, cursed with losing teams but blessed with pure panache. In his years with the New Orleans Saints, he was the toast of a high-toasting town, and he continues to be revered in his adopted city, now working as a corporate spokesman for a variety of companies.

He married his college sweetheart and the Ole Miss Homecoming Queen, Olivia, and together they had the three boys. The first one, Cooper, weighed in at 12 pounds, 3 ounces. Peyton was 12 pounds, 1 ounce. "Eli weighed right in at 10 pounds," the father says. "So we thought something might be wrong with him."

Not surprisingly, all of them became outstanding athletes. Archie Manning passed on his football talent to his sons. He also made time for them, playing ball with his boys in the yard. "He didn't have real good mechanics," says Eli. "He'd say, 'Don't do this like I did, that's wrong.' He was just a good athlete." For all his time and all his skills, though, Archie never pushed his sons to follow him into the National Football League. "He never forced us to play any sports," continues Eli. "When I was 11, I didn't want to play baseball anymore. That was fine with him. If I had said I didn't want to play football, that would have been fine too."

But the kids took to football. And Archie wouldn't leave them alone when it came to dragging them along everywhere—to ballgames, to practices, to banquets where his were the only children. "He didn't think anything of bringing us anywhere," recalls Cooper. "I know he took us places we didn't have any business being. He was just like, 'If we're coming, they're coming.' We were just part of the gang. We'd be at little parties running around, the only kids there. I think he got kind of a kick out of us. Maybe not when we were 1 or

2, but when we were 3 or 4. When we were 3, we were riding shotgun out to practice with him."

"Being a football player is a great job for spending a lot of time with your kids," Archie says, perhaps contrary to popular perception. "You basically work for six months, and the other six months you're on your own. Even during the season, your hours aren't that bad. Cooper, especially, I took everywhere. Nobody was ever going to accuse me of not spending a lot of time with my kids. How many times have parents with kids warned that they're gone before you know it? Well, I *heard* that."

The time he spent with his father as a child was especially helpful to Peyton when he faced the pressure of the media swarm and fans at the University of Tennessee and now in Indianapolis. He is unfailingly polite, as good with the media as with his fans—even after the first couple of games of his rookie year, when he was struggling. "What I remember about watching my dad when I was little is, everything he did, he did with class," Peyton says. "He'd sign a lot of autographs, really spend a long time doing it, and he did it whether he won or lost. It takes a few seconds to sign an autograph, and if it makes someone happy, why not just take those few seconds? I learned that from him. And I learned from him that if you're going to do interviews after you score four touchdowns, you better do them when you throw four interceptions."

Although Peyton is now signing autographs, Cooper, two years older, was the first real hope Archie Manning had that one of his sons might follow him in the NFL, although Cooper also says that while his father pulled for him, he never pushed him into football. Cooper went to Ole Miss to play receiver but had to give up football when doctors discovered a congenital spinal defect. They told his parents that with

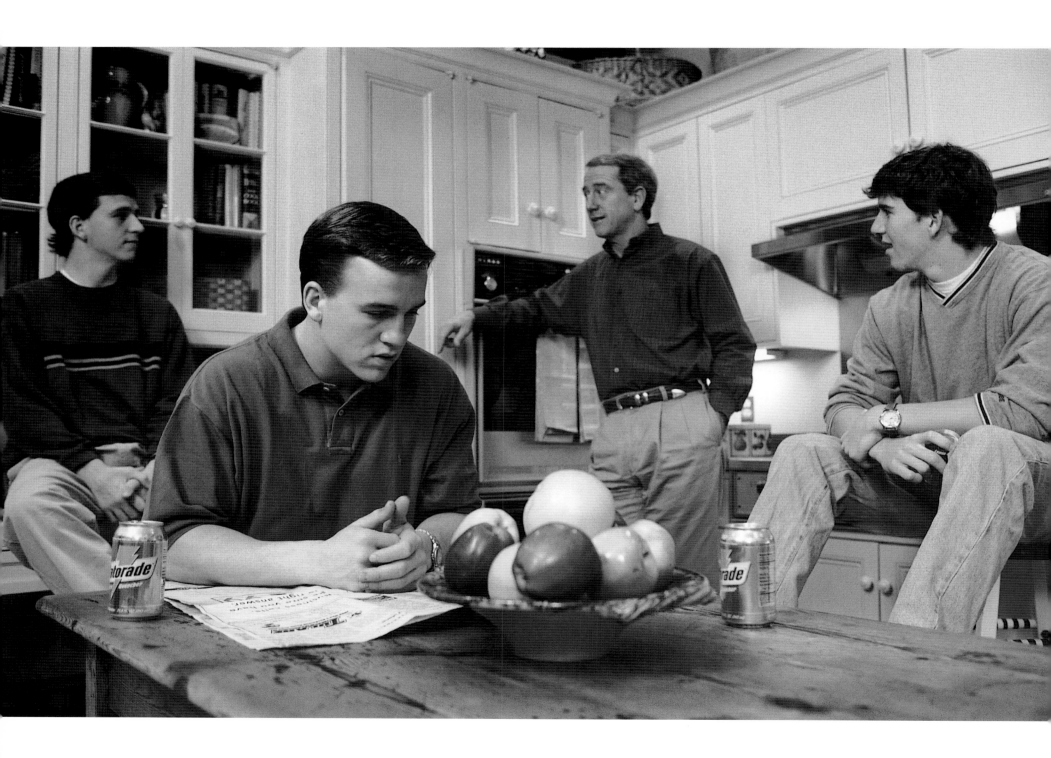

all of those hits in all of his years of football, it was a near-miracle that he wasn't crippled. At first, Cooper was told he needed surgery. Then he was told he couldn't play football again. Then that there was a risk of paralysis. He's fine now, but those football days to come never came. "That was something my dad and I definitely handled together," Cooper recalls. "We traveled to doctors in different cities. The doctors pretty well broke it to me but Dad was there to help me through it. We were at the Mayo Clinic in Rochester, Minnesota, and it was just the most depressing place on earth, and it was snowing, and my dad says to me, 'We have to get out of this town.' We went to the Vikings-Detroit Lions game. He let me drink a few beers with him, anything to get a little life into me."

"The way Cooper handled it," says Peyton, "really helped us all. I'm not saying it wasn't rough, but it just drove home all the more that everything's not football." Adds Archie: "We weren't blowing smoke when we told people football wasn't our number-one priority, and when Cooper needed his surgery, that kind of proved it. We were so grateful that this thing was discovered so we could get him off the football field. This was serious, and we wanted our son more than we wanted a football player."

With Cooper on the sidelines working sales and marketing in the oil business and Peyton secure in the NFL, Eli is now stepping into his own. The nation's top colleges heavily recruited him. There was pressure to follow Peyton's footsteps at Tennessee. There was pressure to attend his father's college. And wherever he would end up, there would be pressure to be as good as they were in their college days.

"Peyton had his great career and my dad had his great career," Eli says. "I can't help that. I can't be blamed if I'm not as good as them. I can only be myself and do the best I can. There's only one Heisman Trophy winner and only one first pick in the draft. I'm going to have fun playing football, fun going to school. If I get in the NFL, fine. If I don't, I'll get a regular job and be a regular working man and that'll be fine." He insists neither his brothers nor his parents pushed him to one college or the other, including Ole Miss, "But maybe deep down," he admits, "Mom wanted me to go there."

Archie Manning thinks his youngest son will handle the pressure just fine. Just like his two brothers have. The father's aware of how fortunate he is. Other fathers, he knows, have raised their children with love and have been disappointed. "You know, I've always been reluctant to give advice on being a dad," he says. "With Peyton's fame over the years, I've been asked to give some talks on parenting and family values and things like that. I was reluctant to wear that hat. I have a problem getting up in front of a lot of folks and beating my chest and saying, 'I've conquered the parenting thing.'"

"On the other hand," he adds, "maybe it's pretty simple. You've got to love your kids, you give them quality attention, and you just pray that you'll be lucky. Stick with them. I try not to smother my kids. I love being with them, but I happen to be a lot older than them. They're in their twenties, and if I can't go with them somewhere, I understand that. I let them go. I know they're good guys, and that's enough for me. That's all I ask of them. When I look back, that's all my daddy asked of me—to be a good guy."

The Mondavis: Robert, Michael, and Tim

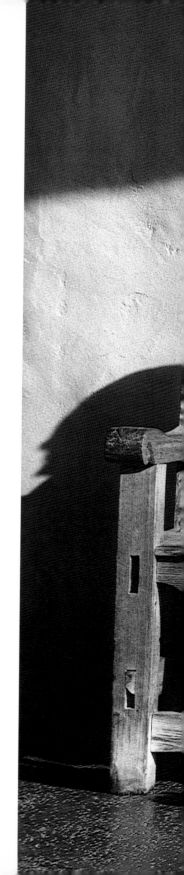

The question, over time, became clear to Robert Mondavi: How could he be reasonably certain that his children would be able to sustain the business that he began in 1966, the business that helped transform the wineries in California's Napa Valley, and Mondavi wines in particular, into some of the world's finest?

In 1990, Robert took a step—just a step—toward answering that question, inching into the background as he began to pass control of his enterprise to his sons, Michael, the elder, and Tim. It was a tricky transition and not exactly a smooth one. After all, how does a father decide which of his sons would take control of a storied and multimillion-dollar business?

Robert decided he'd put them both in charge.

And almost immediately, the tension between the brothers grew like vines.

Says Michael: "Our personal relationship kind of evaporated. We developed into a business run by a family, but we were not a family running a business." Except for work-related issues, the brothers rarely spoke. They

From left, Michael, Tim, and Robert Mondavi at their winery in the Napa Valley.

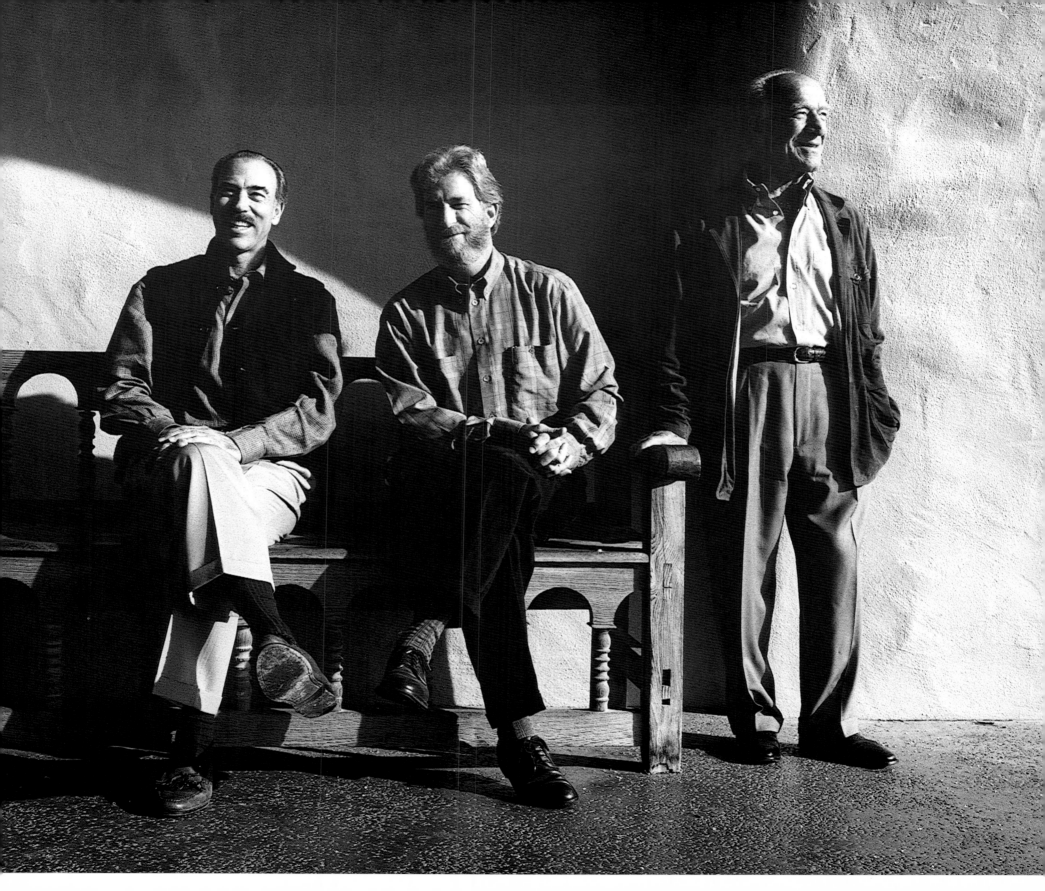

And in that blind test in France, two of the winning wines were produced by former assistants at the Mondavi winery. "We kind of refer to ourselves as the University of Mondavi," Michael explains of his family's support for Mondavi winery alumni. "The experience they garnered with us enabled them to do what they do—and do it very well."

Now that he had proved what was possible, Robert was more energetic than ever in improving his wines, building his company.

The results have exceeded even Robert's lofty expectations. The family business now produces wine in California, France, Italy, and Chile. And Robert still works more than a full workweek, often on the road, using his name and his story to hawk his wine around the world.

But what about the future? Five years after the experiment of co-CEOs began, both Michael and Tim approached their father. It wasn't working, they told him. Decisions were being put off because nobody was clearly in charge. "We would debate things and never come to conclusions because one of us wouldn't convince the other, there wouldn't be unanimity, and therefore no decision would be made," Michael says. "We were a ship without a rudder."

So Robert sat down with both of his sons in an office at his winery, defined by the mission-style arch and bell tower that has become the company logo. Michael was eight years older, and Robert decided he would become sole CEO. Rather than proclaim victory, Michael put his brother in charge of the actual grape growing and wine making, areas that had always been Tim's passions.

"I picked and I was relieved," Robert recalls. "I'd been stalling, and I was hoping as they got older they'd realize they need each other. I knew they had enough common sense that it would work out. I also saw how hardheaded they were, and they weren't using common sense. But then it dawned on them, by God, they were both wrong

and they were both right."

"My father, because of his experience at Charles Krug, was concerned if he picked one son for CEO, he'd lose the other one," Michael says. "But if you want a growing company to stagnate, you set up an office of co-CEOs. That'll kill things. It certainly wasn't helping us."

"It wasn't working the way it was," Tim agrees, adding that he has never been bitter about his father's decision. It made sense, he says, and it is working. "I'm very happy with what I'm doing and with how the company is doing."

The family is doing better as well. They talk more. The tension has evaporated. The brothers have reconciled.

And, as with wine, time has improved Robert's relationship with his sons. While Robert's "hobbies, avocation, and vocation" were once solely the wine business, Tim says, he has changed. Robert is now more than a boss.

"In the past five years, my boss converted to being a mentor and a father," Michael agrees. "He's more thoughtful, maybe more considerate, and rather than focusing on himself, he has focused on helping others, in helping them find themselves."

Robert admits he could have spent more time being a father, less as a businessman. But not without paying a price. "I don't think we could have done anything else," he says. "We're so focused on this wine business lock, stock, and barrel. It might be a mistake, I don't know. But I know we couldn't have done what we did without that focus."

Besides, he adds, things have turned out just fine. The business is thriving. And there's more.

"I'm at ease with myself," he says. "My sons are talking to each other, working as a family unit. Now we have harmony and common sense. I'd say that's not bad."

The Thomases: Richard, Rich, and Montana

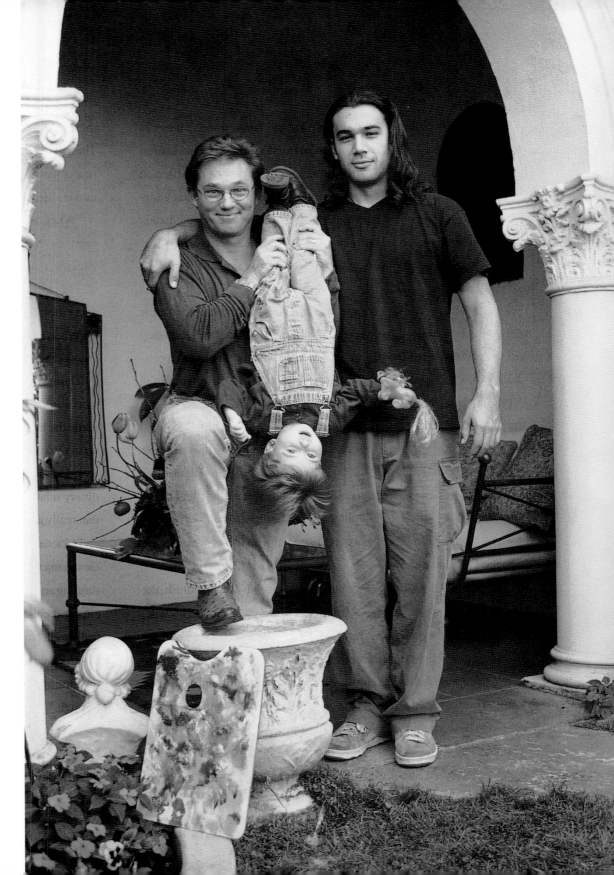

Richard Thomas and his sons Montana (upside down) and Rich.

ichard Thomas calls it "The John-Boy Thing." Never mind that he has produced lavish stage productions of *Hamlet*. Or that he has starred in *The Count of Monte Cristo* to rave reviews. Forget that he has directed Stephen Crane's *The Red Badge of Courage*. When people see his wide-grinning face with the ashen birthmark on his cheek, what immediately comes to mind is the CBS classic, *The Waltons*. And "The John-Boy Thing" kicks in: "Hey, John-Boy!" people still yell to Thomas after all these years. "How's Mary Ellen?"

You know why. *The Waltons* was the Thursday night television staple that guys used to make fun of but could not keep from watching. John-Boy was the earnest, sensitive guy, who—had his character not been so convincing and real—was almost out of place in a 1970s show set in the Depression era. The show was as culturally engrained as any before it and any show since. And so . . . "Hey, John-Boy!"

"It can get a little tiring," Thomas admits from his five-bedroom house in the Los Feliz section of old Hollywood. "But it's not like *The Waltons* was a show I was embarrassed about or that John-Boy was a character I didn't like. If that were the case, it might really bother me. But it was a good, quality show and John-Boy was a good character who I was very proud of. In fact, it was a great show."

Thomas's life after Walton's Mountain might resemble, at first blush, the show he starred in for five seasons before leaving in 1975. He and his wife, Georgiana, now have the same number of children his television parents had—seven—and they are exceptionally close. Midwives delivered the most recent addition to the family, his son Montana, at home. ("At one point," Thomas recalls, "Georgiana was in extreme pain and she said, 'I want to go home.' I said, 'Honey, I don't know how to break this to you, we are home.'")

Beyond that first blush, though, Thomas's family is non-traditional to the bone. The seven children are products of several marriages: In Thomas's first, he had his eldest child, Richard Francesco, as well as identical triplet daughters; his current wife, Georgiana, brought two more girls into his life; and together they had Montana in 1996.

"When we all moved in together it was like a solar system coming together," recalls Thomas, rolling his eyes behind his wire-framed glasses, which are similar to the specs he wore as the eldest Walton. "I mean, a whole race of dinosaurs was probably destroyed by an event like this. I never thought that I'd be in what people would call a non-traditional family. When I was married the first time, I thought that was it. But here I am. I was dragged kicking and screaming into a better life."

Thomas's divorce from Rich's mother was not easy on his eldest son, who was in high school at the time. The father and son, though, not only made the best of it, but found themselves closer as a result. "When there wasn't that significant other around, we'd go to dinner, he took me to an awards show, it was great," Rich recalls. Says his father: "It was an extraordinary relationship. He was a teenager and I was a single guy again, and that really gives you time to meet your son. It was precious."

Precious though it may have been, it could not last forever. Thomas met Georgiana while he was doing theater in Scottsdale, Arizona, and she was running an art gallery. They were married in November 1994, and the parents and children moved in together in Los Feliz. "The blending went really well. Not without its rough periods, but really well," Thomas recalls. "I think it was toughest on Richard because he was away at college a lot of the time and really didn't have that full kind of bonding that we all went through."

"Sometimes when I came home," recalls Rich, "it felt like I was walking in during the middle of a movie. I had to keep asking everyone what's happened so far. But I'm totally psyched at the way things are working out."

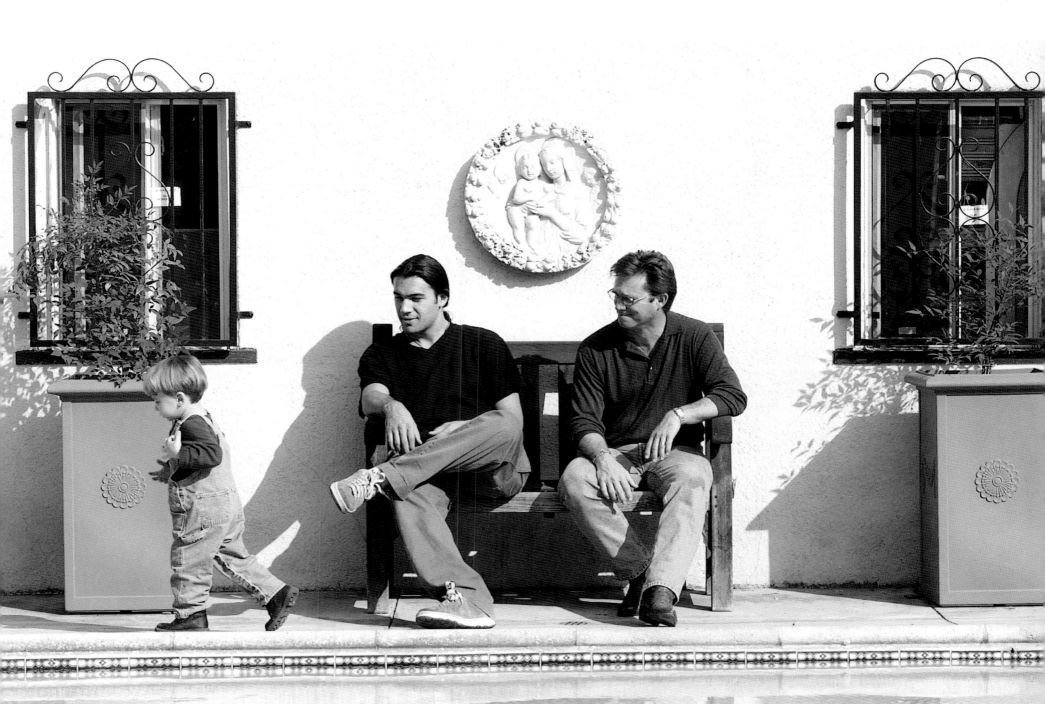

In 1995, things worked this way: Thomas, at 41 and with his first son already in college, decided with Georgiana to have a baby together.

"We were debating back and forth whether we should have another child, because we would basically be indentured for a long, long time," Thomas says. "But I've found being an older dad to be one of the best things that could happen to someone. I would recommend it to any older man, as long as they're spry enough, you know, to pick the kid up and carry him around. For one thing, the anxiety level is a lot less now about everything. I know he's going to have anger, he's going to be aggressive, and he's going to work through that. It's almost like I'm a different person having this son, but the only real difference is I know more and I have a whole new opportunity to make mistakes."

The brothers, at first, had difficulty bonding. Montana, after all, was a baby, and Rich was in college. "But we've had our bonding moments," says Rich, who, like his father's most famous character, is an aspiring writer. "I took him to the zoo. If you really want a kid to love you, do that. He was pointing at every animal and holding on to me, and he just loved that I took him there.

"It'll be interesting later because when I'm around my dad's age, Montana will be about my age now," Rich says. "With my dad, we still had that father and son thing, but we couldn't let the roles get mixed up. It'll be different for Montana and me. When we're that age, he'll still be my brother and we won't have to worry about stepping on any psychological booby traps. We can keep that same relationship going."

It has been more strange than trying for Rich to grow up the son of one of the country's more recognizable faces. He went through a phase where people referred to him as "John-Boy Junior." A bitter teacher once told him she didn't care if his father were Richard Thomas or Jesus Christ; that she would not be treating him any differently than the other students.

"And one time," recalls Rich, "my girlfriend was like, 'I about had a crush on your dad.' Now, *that's* different."

"One of the worst things about fame," says Thomas, "is for your wife and kids because it alters how people behave. They'll come up to my wife and say, 'Nice to meet you.' Then to me it's, 'Oh, it's *really* nice to meet you.' It's kind of blinding in a way."

Rich grew up after the John-Boy era, after the show's weekly close—"Good night, John-Boy; good night, Elizabeth; good night, Jim-Bob—became a bedtime giggle to brothers and sisters all over the country. Which is not to say Rich is oblivious to just how much a part of Americana his father's character was—and is. While Thomas continues to perform theater, star in television movies, and make the occasional guest appearance on today's shows, "The John Boy Thing" will always be there, and Rich is smart enough to know that is because of the power of the character. Little Montana may know as well some day, both because of reruns and because of the stories that people continue to share with his father.

Stories like this one. "I was doing the *Fifth of July* on Broadway," Thomas explains, "and after one show, this Vietnam veteran comes up to me and tells me, 'You know, I was a POW in Hanoi, and at night, when it was time for sleep, me and the other prisoners would do that whole thing, that 'Good night, John-Boy; good night, Jim-Bob.'

"Well, I thought that was real nice," Thomas says of the veteran's story, "but then this prisoner—this POW—he says to me, 'You know, when we were doing that 'Good night' stuff, we did it because we all missed home—and because sometimes that was the only way we would know who was still alive.'

"I hear stories like that," says Thomas after a pause, "and it's a character I can live with."

The Pettys: Richard, Kyle, and Adam

Richard Petty surrounded by his son Kyle and grandson Adam at the TranSouth 400 in Darlington, South Carolina.

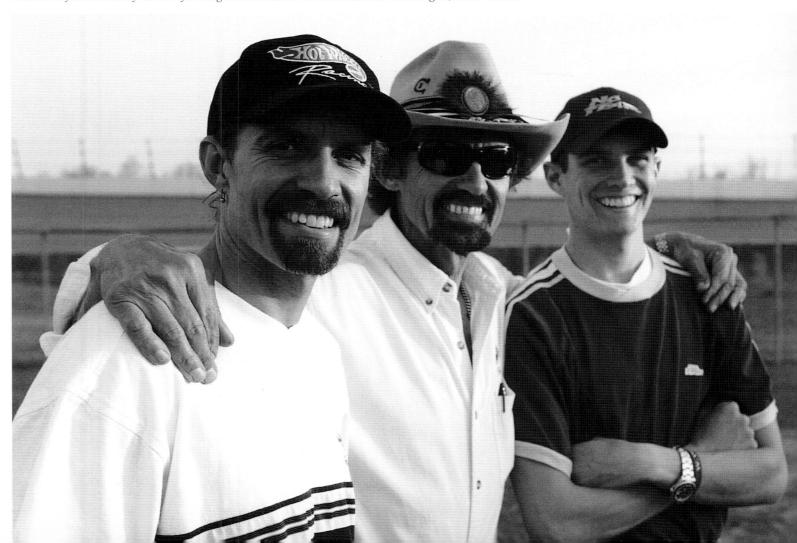

In NASCAR circles, they are considered royalty, a reign rooted in 1949. That's when Lee Petty drove in the organization's very first race, eventually motoring his way to NASCAR titles in 1954, 1958, and 1959, and to his Hall-of-Fame status as one of the best drivers in history.

The greatest of all time, though, is his son Richard—the "King" as he is known—the toothy, mustached legend who's most recognizable under a large feather-adorned cowboy hat and behind dark wraparound shades, sporting a belt buckle slightly larger than a hubcap. He has 200 NASCAR victories under that belt and is, indisputably, the man who set the standard for success in the sport.

And now Kyle and Adam Petty are competing in professional racing. Kyle, Richard's son, became the third generation of Pettys to find success on the Winston Cup circuit, cruising up on double-digit victories in NASCAR's major league. And Kyle's son, Adam, who took the wheel in 1999 at the Busch Grand National Series, NASCAR's minor league, is the only fourth-generation athlete in the United States to compete full time in any major sport.

"It makes you real proud that they thought enough of our business to follow in our footsteps," says Richard, speaking for himself and his father, who stopped doing interviews in the mid-1990s. "'Course, they been around racetracks since they were born. This is the only life they know."

The life they know today includes potential winnings of millions of dollars, in large part because of a boom in NASCAR's popularity that was fueled by the King as much as anyone. Far from the days when men—and some women—would race their family cars on isolated dirt tracks in the Southeast, NASCAR has become the fastest-growing professional sport in the United States, and its popularity shows no signs of running out of gas.

Although Richard retired from competition in 1992, racing is still the life he knows best. (He made a run for Secretary of State in North Carolina in 1996, but his campaign faltered partly because he was accused of using a NASCAR-type move on Interstate 85—bumping a car ahead of him that was dawdling in the speed lane.) His company, Petty Enterprises, still fields two Winston Cup teams and one in the NASCAR Craftsman Truck Series. As a result, Petty remains a familiar figure at the racetracks. And in Adam's first season, twenty-two of his Busch Grand National races ran on Saturdays at the same tracks as the Sunday Winston Cup races in which Kyle competed for Petty Enterprises, so the three generations were together often.

Off the track, they work on cars together at the family's business in the North Carolina Piedmont, get together for dinner and talk cars, sit on the porch and talk cars. But all of the Pettys say racing has never overtaken their family life. Instead, it's driven them to greater honesty with one another and to an appreciation for life that comes when you see your father, your grandfather, your son, or your grandson flying around an oval at more than 200 miles per hour with little more than thin sheet metal and prayers for protection. They certainly don't dwell on the dangers on the racetrack, but neither are they unaware that cars, asphalt, and speed can add up to tragedy. Perhaps that's why they're so close, why they talk so often.

"We'll talk about other stuff, even if it comes back to racing a lot of the time," Richard says. "If you had to rank them, family comes first, racing comes second. This just happens to be what we do."

"I don't think it ever strains things," adds Kyle, once undecided about whether to go into driving cars, racing motorcycles, or singing country music. "If you have a bad day at the racetrack, I think a father and son are family and can say things—just bare honesty—that you

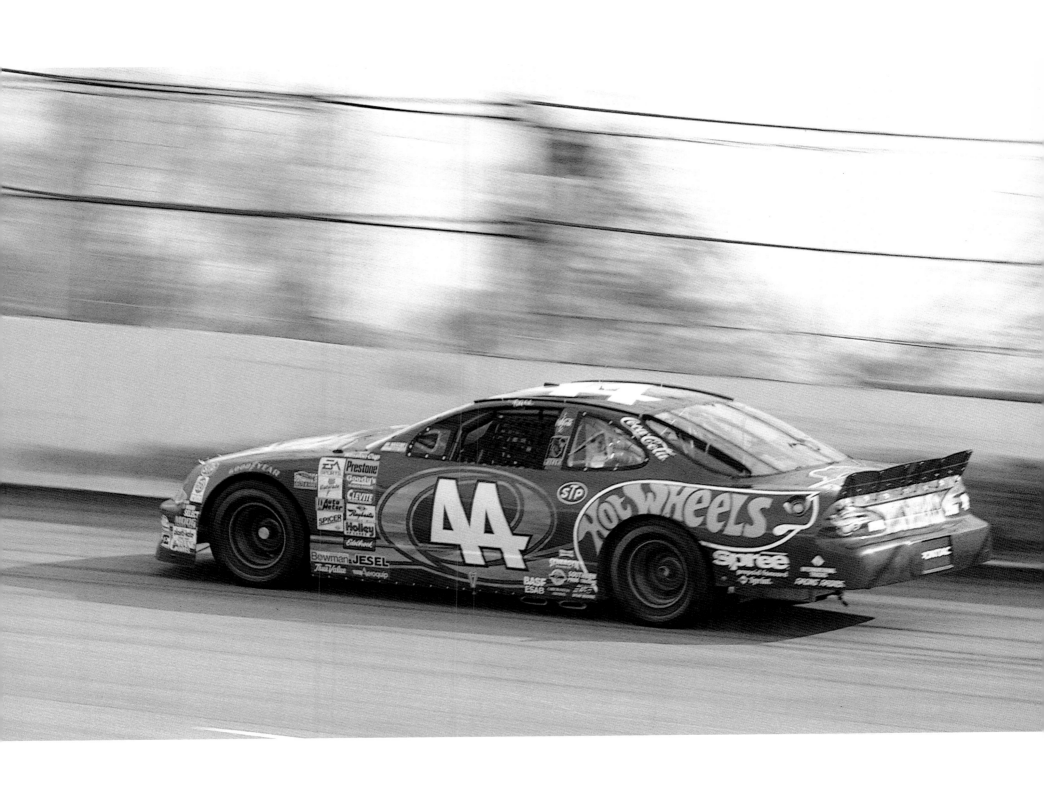

couldn't say to someone else, like 'You were terrible,' or 'You have to pick up the pace.' Or a lot of times if we've had a problem on a race, we just cut right through to the heart of the matter. Is it the driver or the car, the engine or the crew? We don't have to beat around it for fifty minutes or an hour."

That honesty extends to their personal lives, they add, so the communication lines are always open. If a Petty is feeling down in the mouth or gets up in arms, there is always someone to give advice or help even more by merely listening.

"I can talk to my dad about anything," Adam says. "There's nothing I'd ever be afraid to tell him. He's like my best friend." And, he continues, "If he's not around, I can talk to my grandfather."

Both Adam and Kyle grew up in the infields of Winston Cup racetracks, so they have always had the same primary interest, helping to strengthen their bond. But Adam and his father differ in at least one respect. While Kyle grew up uncertain about what he wanted for a career, Adam knew since he was a young boy that he wanted to follow in the Petty footsteps. "I started racing go-karts when I was six," he says. "I guess I was hit by the bug. All I've ever wanted to do is race."

Ironically, the most successful racer in the family, King Richard, was the one who had some childhood years that didn't involve NASCAR. He was 12 when the organization was born. Lee, the family patriarch, began his career late in life compared to the generations that have followed him. In 1948, at the age of 35, he and his brother raced a rebuilt 1937 Plymouth and won the first event they entered. When NASCAR was born a year later, Lee raced a 1948 Buick under the new rules of the "strictly stock" division. He crashed but would quickly get his bearings as a racer, and from 1949 to 1959 he finished no lower than fourth.

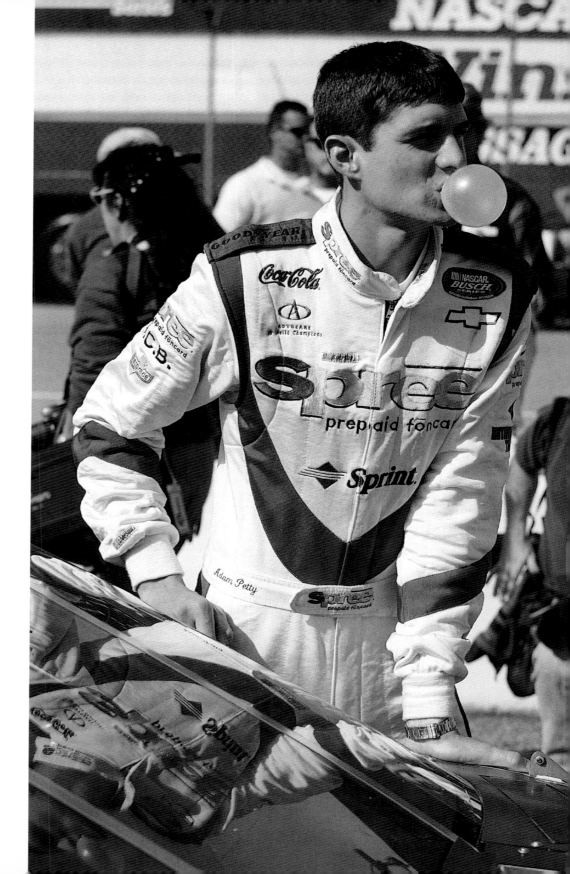

"It was so primitive when it began, all of us learned it as it evolved," Richard recalls of NASCAR's earliest days. "Me and racing grew together. By the time Kyle got there, racing was like a teenager. Now that Adam's there, let's say racing's in its fifties. It's not old yet."

If Richard faced the pressure of being Lee's son, and Kyle faced even more pressure as Richard's son, Adam has had to follow three successful careers. Still a teenager, the weight of that family name on his back could feel like one of the trucks his father's team races. But he won't let it.

"You could say people put more pressure on me because of who my family is, but I'm not putting that pressure on me," Adam says, relaxing after successfully qualifying for a race at Darlington Speedway in South Carolina in front of his father and grandfather. "I'm just a kid having fun with a job that makes me go around in circles at 200 miles per hour."

Richard says he rarely worries about Kyle racing and Kyle claims he seldom worries about Adam on the track, but they know zipping around the racetrack can be dangerous. Richard had a serious accident at Darlington when Kyle was just a kid, and the risks they face every weekend aren't lost on the family. In fact, Adam has had to deal with the sometimes grim reality of racing in the most brutal of ways. It was the summer of 1998, and Adam was driving at the Minnesota State Fairgrounds. On a routine pit stop, his crew chief, Chris Bradley, had gone under Adam's car while it was up on a jack. When the jack was lowered, Adam was signaled to go, nobody realizing that Bradley was still under the car. He was killed.

Adam says he had trouble recovering from the accident, but it's given him a greater appreciation for danger at the track—and he says it made him closer to God and his family.

"I probably should think about Adam's safety more," Kyle admits. "I think I thought about it more the first time I saw him drive a racetrack. But he has so much talent, it's like I'm watching someone who's been driving for twenty years, and then he gets out of the car and it's my kid."

Richard, kicking back atop a trailer at Darlington, crossing his alligator and leather boots, couldn't be more satisfied with his weekends whether Adam and Kyle win or lose. They're good kids, he says, a good grandson and a good son who both respect their elders and acknowledge God in all their accomplishments. Winning or losing a race can't change that.

"Don't get me wrong," Richard says, flashing that picket-fence grin. "I want them to win. But I look at Kyle and I'm proud of the things he's accomplished off the racetrack. He's a great father, he works with kids, and that makes me real proud of him. Adam, he's not that flamboyant with the girls or a kid who runs off at the mouth. He's just a polite kid."

Adam is looking forward to a long, successful career, as is Kyle as he moves into his forties. And Richard, now in his sixties, says he'll be at the racetracks for a lot of weekends to come. "Somebody asked Kyle once, 'When's your daddy going to step away from racing?'" Richard recalls. "Kyle says, 'Where would he step to?' He was right about that."

"Racing's in his blood," Kyle declares. "Racing and his family. It might sound corny or whatever, but at my house, every night before we go to bed, we pray together, still. We all come down, we all gather around the bed, some of us might be laying on it, and we ask God to protect us when we're apart. We always ask for protection for when we travel and as we race. We know we're looked at because we race, and we know how lucky we are as a family. So we pray prayers like that, that we can be humble and be a good influence on peoples' lives."

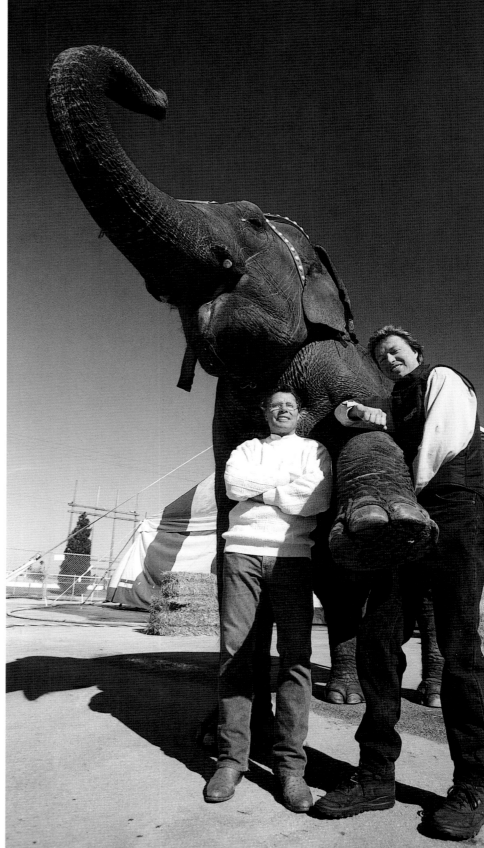

The Gebels: Gunther Gebel-Williams
and Mark Oliver Gebel

From left, Gunther Gebel-Williams and Mark Oliver Gebel with the circus in Florida.

The familiar flowing blond hair is gone from the head and shoulders of Gunther Gebel-Williams. His time in the center ring of Ringling Bros. and Barnum & Bailey Circus is gone as well. No more performing for the muscular man who, beginning in 1949, regularly locked himself in a steel cage with 600-pound tigers and four-ton elephants to become the world's most famous circus performer.

But The Greatest Show On Earth—as it must—goes on.

It goes on with Gebel-Williams's son, Mark Oliver Gebel. He has taken over his father's act, putting on more than 400 shows a year, the father still taking care of the animals but not performing in front of crowds. For Mark, there is the certain danger of being locked in a cage with a dozen Royal Bengal tigers—predators whose most natural instincts are to kill and eat other mammals. But he also has taken on the danger of being compared, always, to his father. Gunther Gebel-Williams is to the circus what Muhammad Ali is to boxing, Michael Jordan is to basketball, Ted Williams is to baseball, and Jack Nicklaus is to golf. Considered the "Greatest Wild Animal Trainer in History," Gunther's snappy and airy movements have been mimicked by trainers who have long stood in the middle of a spotlight yet have never been able to escape his shadow.

That's not a worry to his son.

"I have my father's support, so it's not like I'm in competition with him or what he's done," Mark says. "If other people want to compare us, that's fine for them but not for me. We've been working together all these years. It's not like we're suddenly competing. He's a supporter, not a competitor."

Theirs is a circus family built on support. In their line of work, after all, a support network isn't altogether unnecessary. Imagine it: On the road nearly every day of the year, your co-workers travel-

ing with you. And those co-workers are a bunch of goofing clowns, animated midgets, twisted acrobats, and smelly—sometimes ornery—animals who show their displeasure by kicking, spitting, or biting. Makes the guy at work with the bad jokes and the boring stories seem not so bad.

For this family, though, circus life has been their whole life. It doesn't hurt that they love it. Gebel-Williams was 13 in 1949 when he performed his first solo animal act. When Irvin Feld brought him to the United States in 1968 with the Ringling Bros. circus, his career took off like it was shot from a cannon. So did his personal life. He met his wife, Sigrid. After their marriage, she too performed in the ring with horses and elephants. Together they had Mark, who has been performing since age 4, when he first appeared with elephants. His sister, Tina Gebel-DelMoral, works with elephants, zebras, and horses. And Mark married an acrobat, Cristina Moraru, who later worked with horses as well.

Even with that immersion in circus life, though, nobody could prepare Mark to step in the ring following his father—except his father.

"It was time to get out so that he could take over, and I still could help him," says Gebel-Williams, still a hint of his native Germany in his speech. "When he was growing up, I told him, 'Mark, if you don't want to do it you don't have to do it. You can see I don't have time for anything.' He said, 'No, I want to do it.'"

One of the "anythings" Gebel-Williams didn't have time for was doing the kind of activities with Mark that more traditional father–son pairings do. Mark was always with the circus, of course, so the two were on the road together all the time. "But it was as if I was married to the animals, worrying about them twenty-four hours a day, every day of the year," the father recalls. "You're talking about elephants, horses, tigers. They're very powerful animals, but you have to be there to baby them. If it's cold and the animals are outside, you worry. If it's too hot, you worry."

Says Mark: "He regrets not having more time with me growing up, but that was our life. That can be what the circus is. As far as going out and playing baseball or fishing, we didn't do it. But he's always been a great father. He's just been a different kind of father."

The father and son could not look more different in the ring. Per-

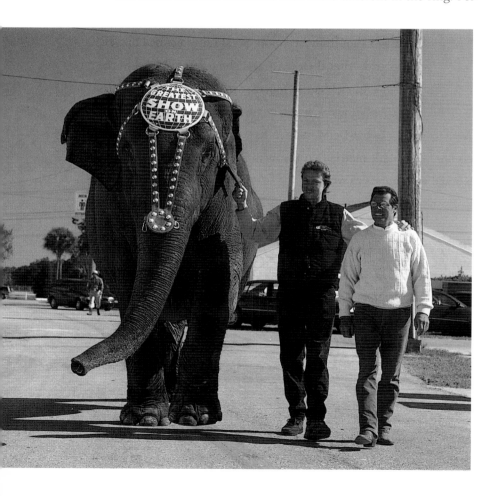

forming into his sixties, Gunther remained stout and muscular, that trademark blond hair cascading down his back. Mark is tall and lithe, his brown hair combed Elvis style. (Gunther only recently went to the shorter, more-natural brown hair. "I started the circus blond," he explains, "and I got stuck with it. I couldn't change it. And every time I would get so upset because I had to set it for thirty minutes to get the color right. I hated that.") What they have in common is their ability with the animals: Not once did a tiger or a lion or an elephant harm Gunther in the ring, and so far Mark has gone unscathed as well. In fact, in more than forty years of performing, Gebel-Williams's most serious circus injury came when someone setting up a tent drove a spike into his foot. Still, he refused to take any time off from the ring.

That's typical of his work ethic. Gunther tried to retire twice. He left the ring in 1990 after a two-year farewell tour, but returned briefly in 1995. He retired again but found himself the only understudy in 1998 when the regular tiger trainer had to leave for a short time for the birth of a child. That trainer was Mark, who gave his father a grandson, Hunter William Gebel.

"I am going to do with my grandson what I never got to do with my son," Gunther says. "I need to learn how to play—what you call?—baseball. I have to do it before he gets too good."

Mark will accept one comparison to his father, he says. If people say he's as good a father as Gunther was to him, he'll be happy. In the meantime, he adds, the comparisons of the two in the ring won't affect him, no matter what the assessment.

"If they compare me and they say I'm better, I would doubt that," Mark says. "If I'm not as good, that's also fine because I'm being compared to my father. That's good enough for me."

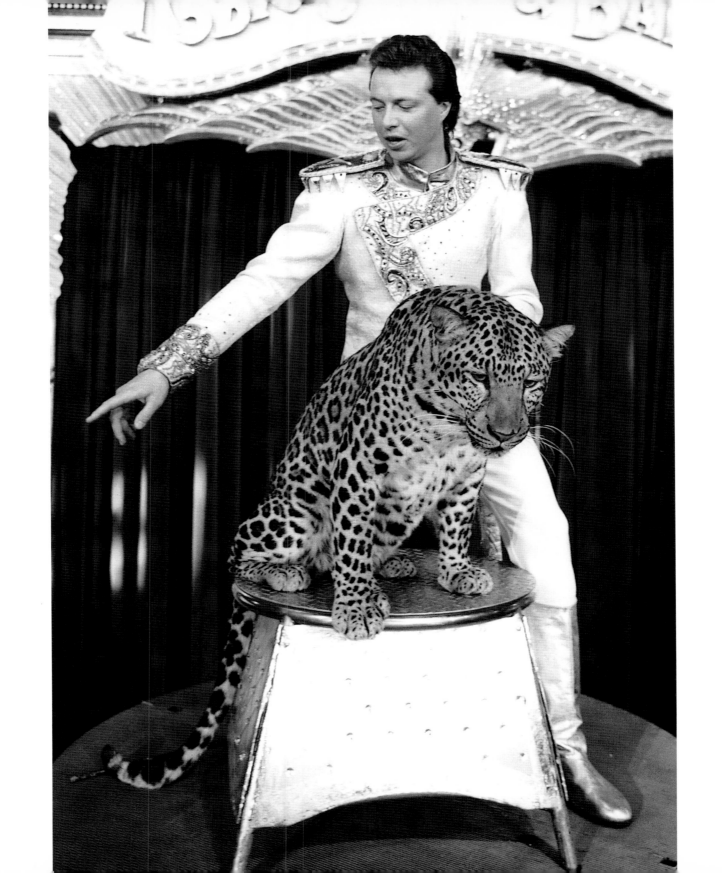

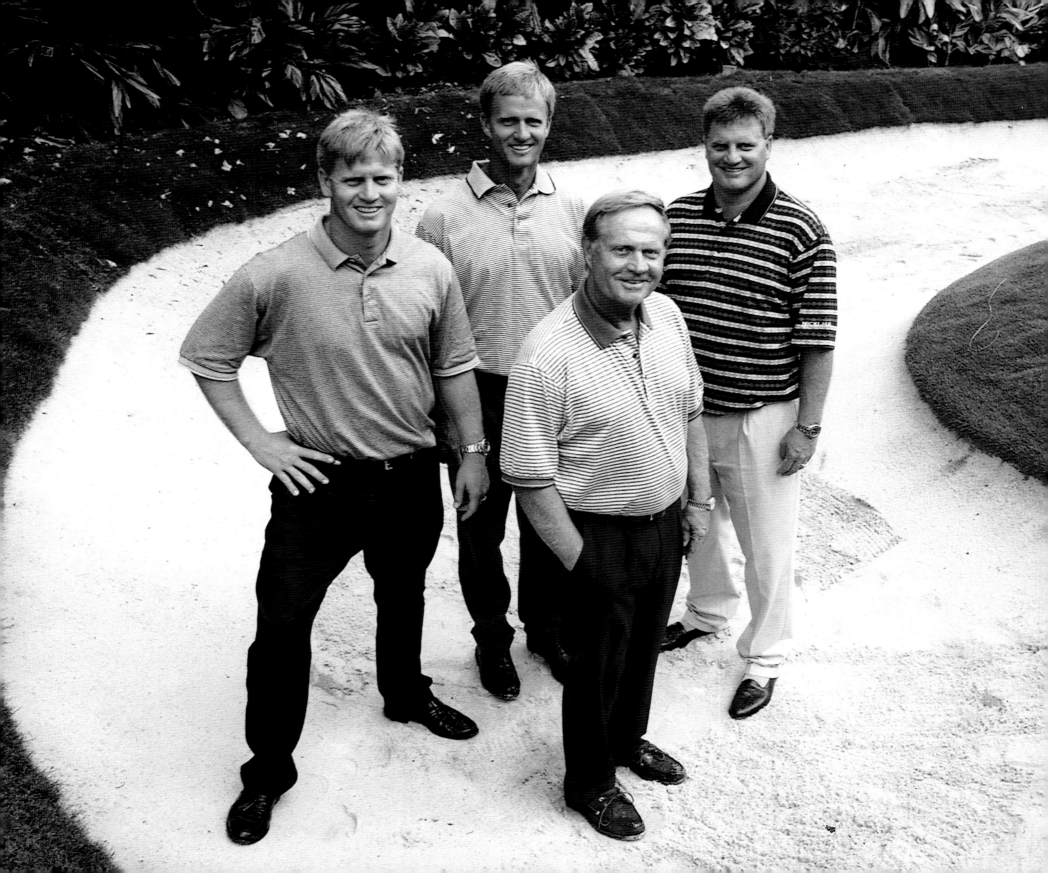

The Nicklauses: Jack, Jackie, Steve, Gary, and Michael

Here's the cold fact: None of Jack Nicklaus's four sons are ever going to be as successful on the golf course as he has been. Another fact: Nobody in the history of golf has been. So it's neither surprising, nor such a tragedy, that the Nicklaus torch to be passed to the next generation will never burn quite as brightly, at least not when it comes to playing golf.

Make no mistake. It's not that Jack's sons are hackers on the links. They're not. Jackie and Steve are strong players, Michael's trying his hand as a pro, and Gary has come into his own, enduring long, solitary trips and tournaments across the country in an effort to make the PGA Tour. His efforts have paid off; Gary recently earned his PGA Tour playing card.

But while Jack may not be able to pass his sweet iron play and clutch putting to his sons, he already has begun to smoothly pass along the family business, which, needless to say, concerns golf. He, his wife Barbara, and the entire family are owners of the Nicklaus/Golden Bear International business, and the

Jack Nicklaus and sons, from left, Michael, Jackie, and Steve in their backyard in North Palm Beach.

sons have gradually become involved in its operations over the years. (Daughter Nan is devoted solely to raising her family, but her husband, Bill O'Leary, is also deeply involved in the company.) Nicklaus/Golden Bear, a multimillion-dollar empire with hundreds of employees worldwide, encompasses golf course design, golf course and real estate development, product licensing, equipment, apparel, golf instruction, television production, publishing, and event management.

All four of Jack's sons have a hand in the business. Some have two.

And all of that means the world to Jack. But so does the fact his sons asked him to be best man in their weddings. And that they all still live within minutes of him. And that, as far as he and his sons are concerned, he did a pretty good job as a father, even as he was wedging in tournament after tournament into a busy family life. Jack Nicklaus and his boys are not just father and sons or mere business partners. They're friends.

That's important to him, in part, because in 1970 Jack lost his best friend—his father. Charlie Nicklaus was only 56.

"I lost him much too early in life," Jack says, sitting at the kitchen table at his home in North Palm Beach, Florida. "He was my best friend, and losing him taught me a few things. One thing it taught me is I wanted to be best friends with my sons."

It taught him a couple of other lessons, too. One was that life doesn't always go on as planned—so you better do what you can when you can. In the last three years of Charlie Nicklaus's life, Jack did not win a major championship. In the years following his death, Jack recommitted himself and won the British Open in 1970, the PGA Championship in 1971, the Masters and U.S. Open in 1972, and the PGA Championship again in 1973.

Aside from the uncertainty of life, the death of Nicklaus's father taught him that if scoring a birdie on a par-3 is tough, life itself is a lot

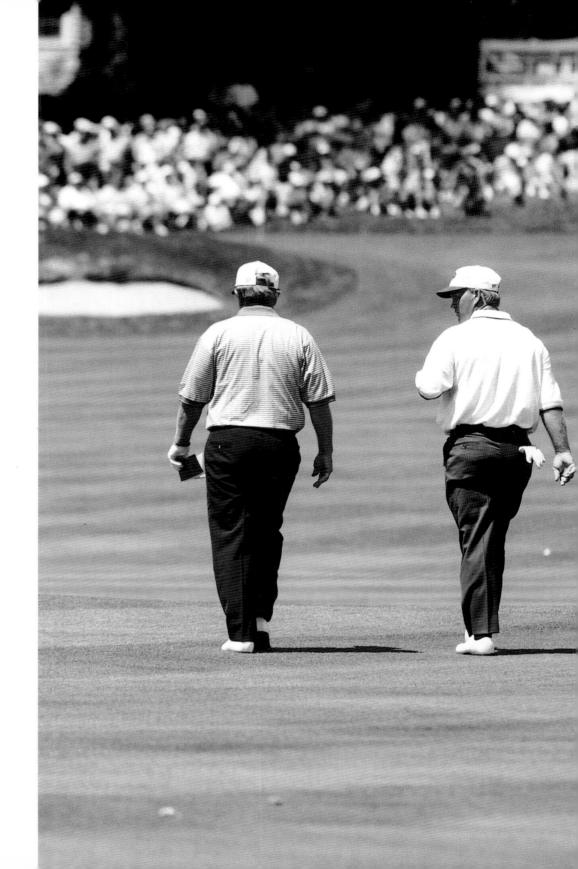

tougher. In life, there are no mulligans.

So throughout his long career, Jack Nicklaus has kept his priorities in order. He didn't try to make it to his sons' football games when he could fit them in around his golf tournaments. He scheduled his golf tournaments around his family life. He still does that, busy as he has been with Golden Bear and the Senior PGA Tour, taking the boys on big-game hunts in Africa, fishing off the coast of their Florida home. It's not enough that they work with him.

"I feel blessed that they want to take part in the company," Jack says. "As far as the business goes, I take them seriously. If they have an idea worth listening to, I listen to it. If not," he adds with a smile, "I take it under advisement—and then I don't do it."

Nicklaus's sons tend to listen to him. Says Jackie, now 38: "I have so much respect for him, and he has this great knowledge that I just want to absorb. Any success I get is a reflection on him."

Steve, 36, agrees: "My father is a very, very smart man."

Jack Nicklaus is also, without rival, the most successful golfer of all time. He has won twenty major championships, including six Masters, five PGAs and four U.S. Opens (all four on Father's Day). He won the British Open three times and the U.S. Amateur Championship twice. In 1986, he ended his remarkable string of victories in the majors when he won his final Masters at age 46, his son Jackie caddying. And now, as he enters his sixties, with a new high-tech hip to replace a faulty old one, he doesn't plan to leave the links anytime soon.

He is, in fact, more involved in the game than ever. He has designed more than 150 golf courses on his own and has more than thirty co-designs and re-designs to his credit. He is widely respected in this area of the industry—his company has had some twenty of the top-100 courses as ranked by GOLF Magazine and Golf Digest.

But how does a father pass greatness onto his sons? Teaching them the technical aspects of any trade or profession is nice, but a lot of that is textbook stuff. Particularly where an artist's eye is required, a father has to move from the technical to the intangible, passing on passion and desire and—perhaps most importantly—confidence to his sons.

Jackie remembers one of those moments. It was way back when he was a kid, just about six years old: "We were in the pool, and I was swimming on his back in the deep end," Jackie recalls. "I was clinging to him and then he just slipped away and let me go. I was flailing, and I had tears in my eyes, and I got to the side of the pool just crying. I'm crying, 'Why did you let me go?' And he said, 'Well, I knew you could swim. You just had to find out.' That's how it's been with course design. My dad had confidence that I could do it, even though I wasn't sure."

Nicklaus's teaching approaches aren't entirely sink-or-swim. Jack, of course, was on hand in the family pool just in case. He remains there for his sons just in case. But he's let them take on their own projects.

And it's in these non-playing roles that his sons may some day match his greatness. After all, this is a second career for Jack. And his sons are starting earlier than he did.

"Whatever they do, I hope they do it well—and I hope they enjoy it," says Jack. "That's what's important to me." He adds, "I don't know that there's a secret other than you get lucky. I give the kids their space. You want them to develop on their own, but at the same time you want to be supportive."

The "Bear Apparent," as he is known in the office towers of Golden Bear, is Jackie, the eldest son, who has now designed ten courses on his own and co-designed nine with his father. Although the sons' positions within Golden Bear's corporate structure are deliberately ill-defined, it's Jackie who has been most hands-on and who has shown the greatest

From left, Jack and his son Gary play as a team in The CVS Charity Classic.

penchant for following in the footsteps of his father's design career. And though he's the first to admit that his golden last name has helped him—and continues to help him—he's already highly respected in the design industry in his own right and gains new plaudits every day.

"I have no doubt that I could disappear tomorrow and Jackie would be very successful," his father says. "He knows what he's doing. They all do, I think. They all have a good head on their shoulders, but they're all different, too—which is the way it should be."

Steve, for example, had been involved in sports management, event management, and even dabbles in course design. Steve's passion the last few years has been a company called Executive Sports International, which manages some forty golf tournaments worldwide. He bought the company from Golden Bear in 1997.

"It's a bit of independence for me," he says. "It was a way for me to get my own company and not have to rely so much financially on my father. But I'd say he's still the boss, even when I'm over here." In addition to turnkey management of events on every tour, Executive Sports International operates the Golden Bear Tour, a successful developmental tour with a lengthy annual waiting list for membership. Steve would like to expand into other sporting venues as well.

Things are a little different for Michael, 26, too. He developed a late passion for golf, but he's still a pro—though he has no serious aspirations of gaining his PGA card. In fact, he devotes most of his energy to developing an Internet startup concept.

Michael clearly demonstrates that confidence in business that his father hoped to instill in his sons, and he gains more every day. But he's also learned from his father's experiences on the golf course, not just when to play it cautious and keep the driver in the bag, but how to handle the pressure and attention.

"With the last name I get some attention in the tournaments, but obviously not like he did," Michael says. "Everybody wants to touch him, talk to him, and he handles every one of them with just as much grace as the last one. It makes me think that whatever attention I get—even though it can be bothersome at times—I can take. Because he's handled so much more so well."

The son who really gets the attention—and faces the pressure—on the links, is Gary, 30. In 1985, he was stuck with the "Next Nicklaus" tag, when *Sports Illustrated* featured him on its cover. Gary was only 16 and there was no real reason to profile him, except that he was the most promising son of a legend. After a 1998 season spent on the European PGA Tour, Gary spent 1999 on the Nike Tour. In 2000, he will play on the PGA Tour. It has been a tough road to get there, though, involving long, lonely drives from one tournament to the next, and extended stretches away from his father and brothers.

Gary, too, realizes that the Nicklaus name can be a mixed blessing. It has gotten him invitations to some tournaments he may not have otherwise played. It's also gotten him a lot of attention, which can be distracting.

"What happens is, where someone named Joe Smith has a bad day and yells at a volunteer and breaks a club, nobody's ever going to think twice about it," Gary says. "But my actions? They reflect on my brothers and sister and mother and father. My father's worked on his image his entire life, and it's up to my brothers and me not to reflect badly on him."

Jack, of course, doesn't know for sure how Gary will do, if he will ever win major championships like he did regularly. He's confident, though, that his son's improving steadily and could be a very good player.

Then again, in one sense, Jack doesn't really care.

He has four smart, healthy sons. They live close to home. He sees them often. He considers them friends, which means more to him than anything. He has learned from his own father's death to take nothing for granted, both on and off the golf course.

"I don't think I gave him 100 percent the last three years of his life," Jack says. "His death really gave me a kick in the rear end, and really made me realize that things aren't forever. I tried not to let that happen to me again. I think that's an important part of what I'm trying to instill in my kids, in everything they do."

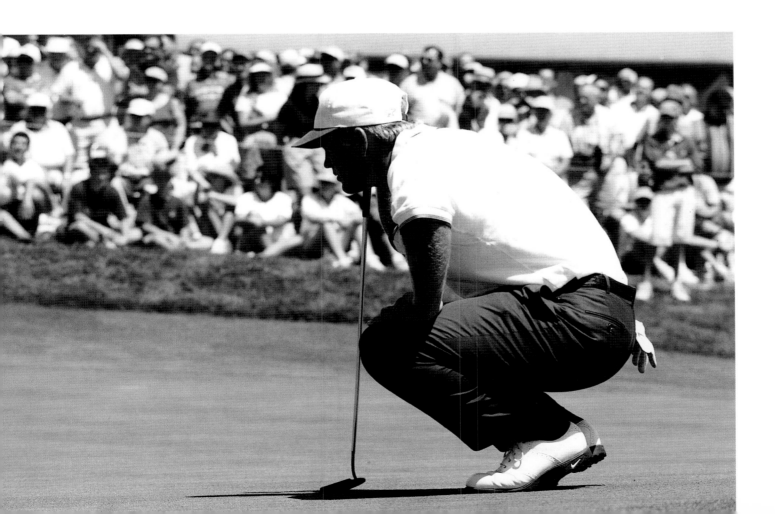

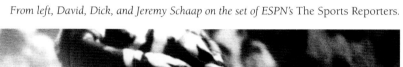
The Schaaps: Dick, Jeremy, and David

From left, David, Dick, and Jeremy Schaap on the set of ESPN's The Sports Reporters.

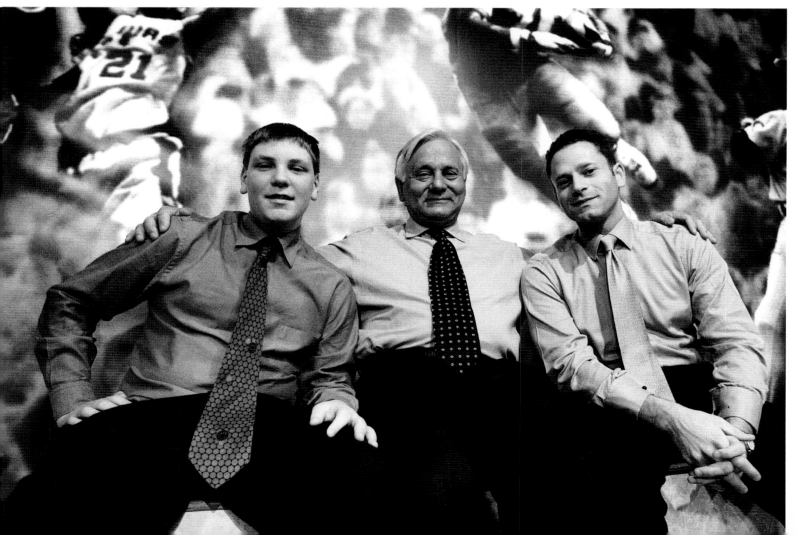

For all his accomplishments as a writer, Dick Schaap's most admiring fans might be expected to put on some pants when he's in their presence. Schaap has written thirty-two books—and counting. Nearly all of them received critical acclaim. In one stretch, he wrote nine books in sixteen months. He once held the title as author of the best-selling sports book of all time, *Instant Replay*, which detailed a year with the Green Bay Packers.

But Dick Schaap's fans? Most of them know him as host of ESPN's *The Sports Reporters*, a weekly show resembling CNN's *Crossfire* but with some of the country's top sports wags discussing the games of our times. The show has become one of the network's most popular, a Sunday ritual for the crowd of groggy, scratching guys who need an early morning sports fix with their coffee. It's a show for the boxer-shorts crowd.

For Schaap, the job is pure bliss, whatever his fans are wearing. He gets to do some writing for the show. He gets to talk sports. And he gets to work with his son, Jeremy, 30, a roving reporter for ESPN and considered one of the network's rising stars.

It's 9:30 on a Sunday morning, and Schaap has just finished directing the traffic of commentary coming from each side of him as he sits in the middle of the set, now a respected elder statesman of the sports broadcasting world.

"This is the closest we've ever been in this relationship," the father says when Jeremy is positioned tightly next to him for a photo shoot.

"And ever hope to be," replies the son.

"I try to encourage his low self-esteem," the father says.

"He's done a great job at that," replies the son.

And on and on with the banter—just like on *The Sports Reporters*—self-deprecating remarks mixed in with shots at each other, always with

affection, the way sports guys tend to do. But they are not shy about praising each other, either, the way fathers and sons as close as they are tend to do.

"I love what I do, and I'm really very, very proud of what he does," Dick says of Jeremy. "And I'm proud not just of what he does but how he does it. He does it with dignity, not looking for the lowest common denominator. There's an awful lot of sports reporting these days that doesn't have the dignity it could have, but he doesn't go that route."

Says Jeremy: "The main thing is, I grew up getting to watch the man who's best at doing what he does. That's the frustrating part, too, because I'll write a script and it's nowhere as good as his. And I think my father is a great father. He also happens to know all the best restaurants when I'm out of town. I'm in Milwaukee and my first call is to Dad, going 'Where do I eat in Milwaukee?'"

David, the younger son, may become a sports personality as well, he says, but at 13 he hasn't quite made up his mind. "I'm thinking maybe a basketball player," he says. "Maybe not." For now he just enjoys rubbing elbows with the famous athletes who seek out his father. Dick has become such an icon of what is right with sports that, while he once had to pursue the athletes, they now look for him.

Just before the 1999 Super Bowl in Miami, for example, heavyweight champ Evander Holyfield came up to greet Dick and David. "We have a Super Bowl party every year, and I got to meet him at Joe's Stone Crab Restaurant," David recalls. "We rented out a private room in the back for our guests. Halfway through dinner he came up to my dad to say hello, and my dad introduced me. I was pretty surprised. Now that was cool."

Jeremy apparently didn't have doubts about his future. At age 8, he was with his father covering Major League Baseball's spring training, and at Dick's urging stuck a microphone in front of Pete Rose and Tommy Lasorda.

"I thought it was on the network," Jeremy says.

"He's still bitching about that one," says Dick.

If Jeremy's first try at broadcasting never quite made it on the air, his father may wish his never did, either. Long respected as a writer, his first blinks into the television cameras were inauspicious. One New York critic had this to say about Dick Schaap, new TV personality: "I didn't think he was going to get through it. Unfortunately, he did."

"In those days, my voice was referred to as raspy. Now it's described as distinctive—even though it's exactly the same," Schaap recalls, not gloating but running a hand through his white hair and smiling. He has learned to roll with the punches. After all, he has thrown a couple himself in his day. When he was a columnist for the late New York *Herald Tribune*, for example, he decided to comment on the firing of Jim Aubrey, a not-very-beloved CBS mogul who was let go the previous day. Schaap wrote: "The friends of James T. Aubrey gathered yesterday to complain about the way CBS treated him, and both of them are very upset."

These days, though, he has mellowed a bit on the air, tending to accentuate the points his panel makes rather than contradict them. He is more a referee and less a boxer (though he is clearly proud of his final words on each show, his "Parting Shot," as the segment is known). He is still writing books, but treasures the time he can spend taking David to sporting events and to the theater. (Schaap is the only person who has a vote for both the Heisman Trophy and the Tony Awards.) He gets to see his older son less frequently, since Jeremy is on the road so often, but Jeremy's travels to the shrines and stadiums of the sports world have made their relationship all the closer.

It was only recently, for instance, that Jeremy first visited Lambeau Field, home of the Packers, a place where his father is as legendary as the Green Bay players he has written about. Schaap's classic *Instant Replay* was co-authored with Packers lineman Jerry Kramer, the right guard whose block opened just enough of a hole for Bart Starr to slip into the end zone to win the Ice Bowl, the 1967 NFL title game against Dallas. Fathers, of course, love it when their sons get the same excitement out of the places and events they did when they were boys, and Schaap couldn't wait to hear Jeremy's reaction, hoping the son would be as excited about it as the father always has been.

"It was awesome," Jeremy says. "I never had a chance to get there. I guess it was good to save it up. I just kind of cruised around the parking lot and people were giving me kilbassa just because of who my dad is."

David, too, appreciates his father's status in the sports world. "I never thought my dad was that big a celebrity, but the more people I meet through him the more I think he is."

Still, what was the most impressed the sons have been their father's fame?

Well, there was that time at the Super Bowl in New Orleans. "Dad was in the middle of a pack of women, signing breasts," Jeremy explains. "That was impressive. That's the first time I fully comprehended his power."

"I was signing stomachs," the father insists.

"I've seen stomachs and I've seen breasts," the son replies. "They were breasts."

And on and on.

The Junes: Harry, Leon, and James

From left, James, Leon, and Harry June in their living room.

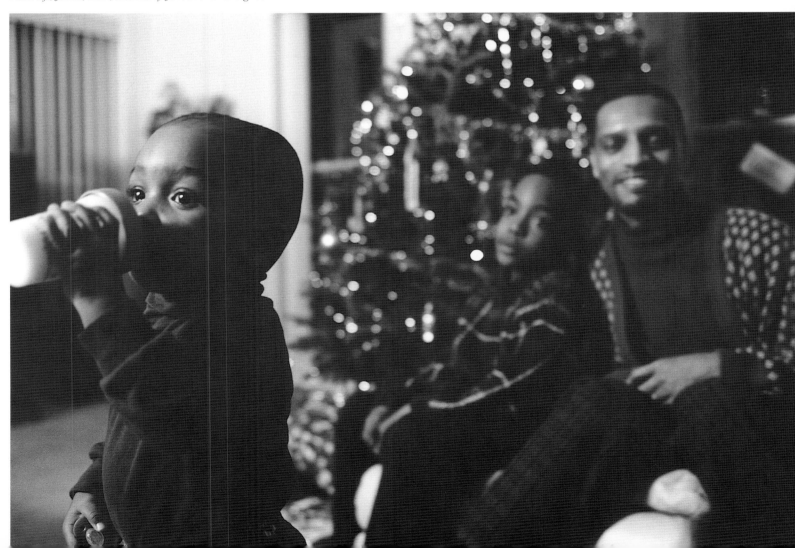

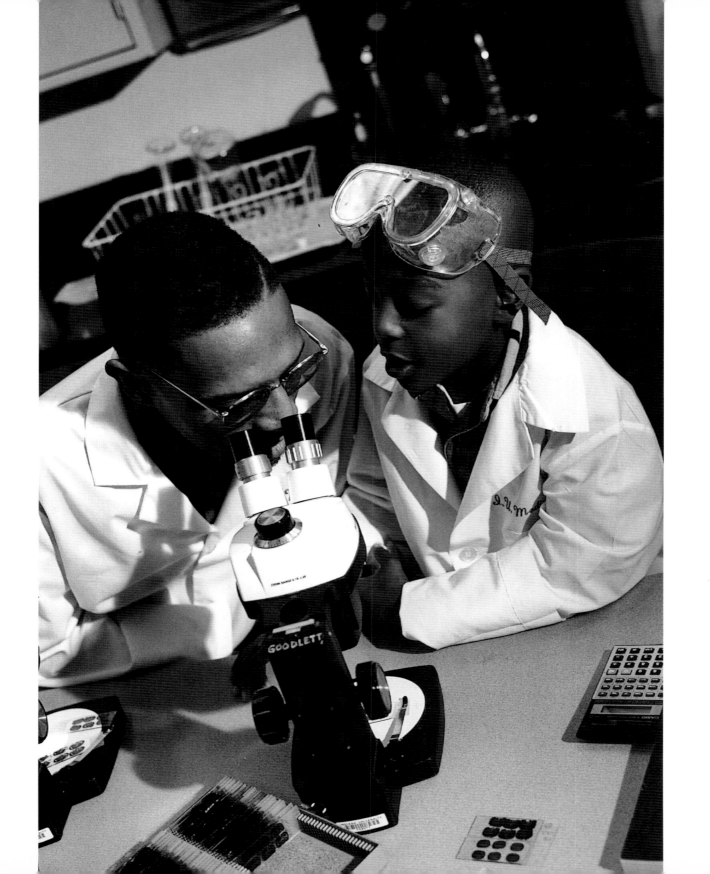

Science is not perfect. And for that, Dr. Harry June, scientist, is grateful.

As one of the foremost researchers on drugs and behavior, working at the Indiana University/Purdue University at Indianapolis, June is looking for a magic pill, one that will combat alcoholism, and he is facing long odds in his search. But June is used to facing long odds—and winning. It was not all that long ago that he was supposed to lose part of his body, maybe his life. It was not much later that doctors told him and his wife, Pamela, to forget about having kids. It just wasn't going to happen, they told them.

Today, Harry has all his body parts, and he is far from dead. He has not just one son but two, Harry Leon June, Jr. and James Franklin. ("My miracle babies," June calls them.) And his research is making great strides. For years, that work took center stage in his life. Now, though, there is James in his crib and Leon, 7, at Harry's side. The older boy wants to toss the football. Or play video games. "I like to play football with my dad," he says. "I like dinosaurs. I like rats." He is all boy. But that he is all anything—that he even *is*—came as a surprise to Harry and his wife, and certainly as a surprise to their doctors.

"I was doing a postdoc, and Pam had been working," June recalls. "After being in school all that time, we decided we wanted to have a family." They tried. Nothing. They waited and tried some more. Nothing. Tests were run. Nothing. More tests. Nothing. And then a cruel conclusion from doctors: "They all but assured us it was just not going to happen."

But research—and thus medicine—can be mistaken in the best of ways, sometimes as miraculously as it can succeed, June knew. In this case, thank God. The doctors were wrong; his wife became pregnant. "To say the least, it's certainly been the most important development in my life—several stages above any research accomplishments that I can ever make. The research accomplishments are not comparable. This is a completely different kind of emotional level."

Later, *in vitro* fertilization would help the Junes have their second child, who for a time they considered as unlikely as their first. "I guess there's some balance to the way things worked out," he says. "They told us Leon wouldn't happen, but then science helped us have James."

While he considers the children miracles, maybe the vagaries—and promise—of science, medicine, and the body should not have come as such a surprise to Harry June. As a young man in graduate school at Howard University he had awakened one morning to find his right shoulder double its normal size. "I knew I was in trouble," he recalls. "This wasn't just some swollen shoulder." Harry was diagnosed with soft-tissue sarcoma in the shoulder. "All things being equal, it was the type of cancer that was supposed to take me out. At minimum, it was supposed to take my arm off.

"I remember when I went to surgery, before I was asleep I said, 'Please don't take my arm off.' I woke up and had a handicapped arm—but I had an arm." He lost 80 percent function in his right hand. No problem. Within two months, he learned to write left-handed. Now, his arm is periodically strapped to a splint because it helps keep his fingers from splaying, giving him increased use when he most needs to use his bad hand. It has been trying. "But it really hasn't been an issue with me mentally," Harry insists. "It's just something I deal with. Especially at the beginning, I just kept my mind on other things. I dove more into my research."

June's research, in a sense, boils down to this: He gets rats drunk, then he opens their brains. So naturally Leon has a few question about his father's work.

"Oh, he wants to know everything," the father says. "Why this?

What's that? On and on." The father answers patiently. And the son apparently listens. "Do you remember why," he asks Leon, "we test drugs on rats?"

"Because," Leon replies, "you don't know if they'll hurt the humans or not."

June does not want to hurt the humans. He wants to help them, just like science helped him have his second son. Thus, the drunken rats with the exposed brains. He is trying to create his own miracle, trying to find a drug that will help people stop abusing alcohol—more effectively and without the side effects that the drugs on the market now carry. To that end, he studies rats that have been bred to have a taste for alcohol.

June does not give the rats little bottles of Jim Beam and sit them in front of a football game. His research is sophisticated, the most advanced of its kind, and it carries all kinds of serious implications for society. The scientific approach to helping alcoholics is different from that of Alcoholics Anonymous, for example. While AA preaches abstinence, June is for controlling the drinking. "We're working on the hypothesis that some people can function as moderate drinkers," he says. "The ultimate goal is to develop compounds to decrease the alcohol that people drink. Think of it as trying to get a pill to stop people from drinking too much."

June has helped discover that alcohol can activate several pleasure centers in the body that are regulated by a variety of neurochemicals within the brain. Maybe that was known intuitively: Get drunk, feel good. But June has played a leading role in identifying a particular brain chemical involved in this process gamma-aminobutyric acid. He refers to it as "GABA." That chemical is of great importance in con-

trolling the pleasure or euphoric feeling obtained from drinking wine, beer, and booze. June helped show that those centers can be activated without the alcohol—but, importantly, drinking alcohol makes that activation easier. "It was a key discovery," he says. "One of the main things we showed is that we could manipulate these pleasure centers."

He proved that by implanting electrodes into the brains of rats, and he explains to Leon, patiently, what he is doing. The rats learned that by pressing on a bar, they would be treated to a pleasurable electrical stimulus. June found that if the rats were given alcohol prior to receiving the electrical current, less current was needed to stimulate the pleasure centers of their brains. June says that because there are so many different types of alcoholics, it is impossible for one medication to work for all of them. To develop new medications, further research is needed on how to isolate the brain's pleasure centers.

Which is bad news for the rats.

June knows how fickle science can be. Knowledge often leads to the need for more knowledge. That is, discoveries lead to the discovery that there's more to discover, and on and on. Occasionally, though, he has learned that while the search never ends, it advances far enough to help people. There's a euphoria that comes along with reaching that point, but even when a lightning bolt strikes in his lab, it doesn't compare to the energy sizzling through his home.

"I can be researching and have a really good day, and it still can't touch being a father," he says. "I can have a really bad day, but to come home and to hear that word— 'Dad'— it just takes it all away. I wasn't supposed to have two sons. I wasn't supposed to have one. So when I hear that 'Dad,' that's the greatest sound in the world to me."

The Rotindos: Marty, Phil, Marty Jr., and Nick

From left, Marty Jr., Nick (kneeling), Phil, and Marty Rotindo strut their stuff.

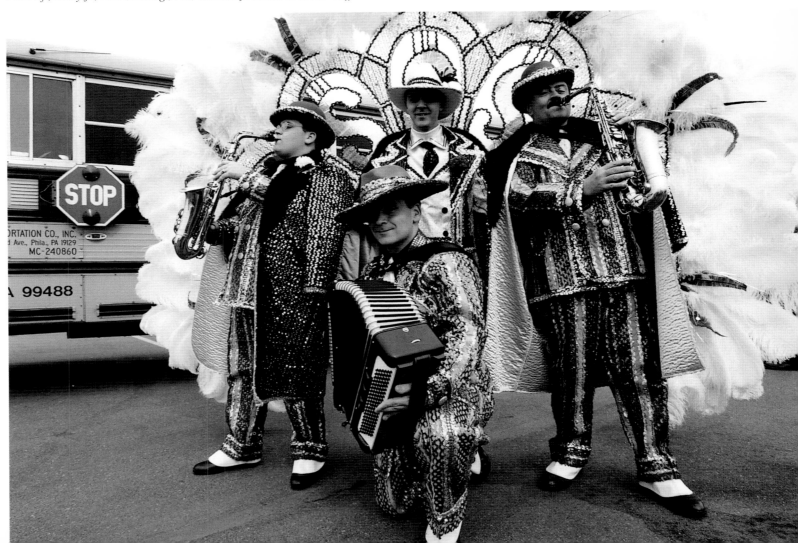

Unless you're from Philadelphia, you've probably never seen the likes of Marty Rotindo and his sons, Phil, and the twins, Marty Jr. and Nick. But in their town, they're as popular as the cheese steak, the soft pretzel, and Rocky.

They are Mummers, a marching, dancing, costumed, instrument-playing band of guys who live for New Year's Day, when they march through the streets of Philadelphia. The annual Mummers Parade, a tradition that goes back a century, regularly draws throngs of people who brave the cold to clap along and high-step it to the spectacle of men wrapped in feathers, lace, sequins, and satin.

For Philadelphia, the Mummers are a phenomenon, a city treasure with a growing national presence. For Marty Rotindo, they're a chance to bond with his three sons, all members of the Ferko String Band.

"I don't think a father could have a bigger thrill than to have three sons who have taken up his hobby," says Marty Sr., decked out in a sequined outfit that clashes like a violent thunderstorm. "It's something that's very, very satisfying."

His high note with the band came when his eldest son, Phil, was elected captain in 1999. At 28 years old, Phil became the youngest captain in Ferko history—no small feat considering the band goes back to 1923 and Phil is only its fifth captain. In his post, he leads the band through the streets, serves as spokesman, and wears magnificently ridiculous costumes as he dances all a-glitter.

On this day, as the band prepares for a performance with "Wiseguys and Jive" as its theme, Phil is in a sequined jacket and pants of black and white stripes, a cascade of gigantic feathers falling from his back. He looks like a cross between a Mafia don and Liberace.

"People call us the Teamsters in feathers," says Phil "Some people don't quite get why we want to do it, and other people couldn't imagine Philadelphia without the Mummers. But what it boils down to for me is it's fun."

His brother Nick agrees. "I think what I like about it is the camaraderie. The whole group is like a bunch of brothers."

The Mummers Parade has its roots in the seventeenth century when Europeans brought to this country their holiday ritual of celebrating the New Year by masquerading, visiting friends and family, and firing weapons into the air. In 1900, the Swedes and Germans of South Philly really felt the party urge, and they strolled through their neighborhoods singing songs, shooting guns, and banging on neigh-

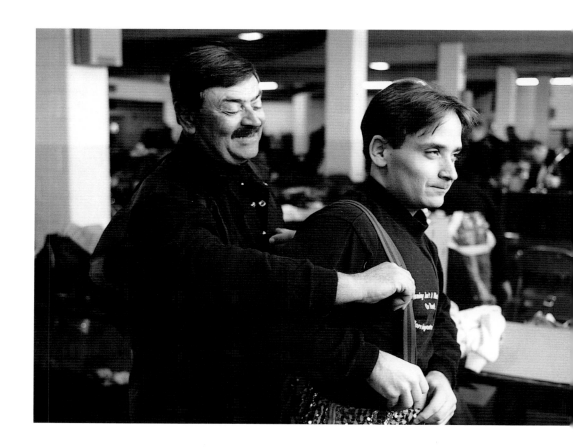

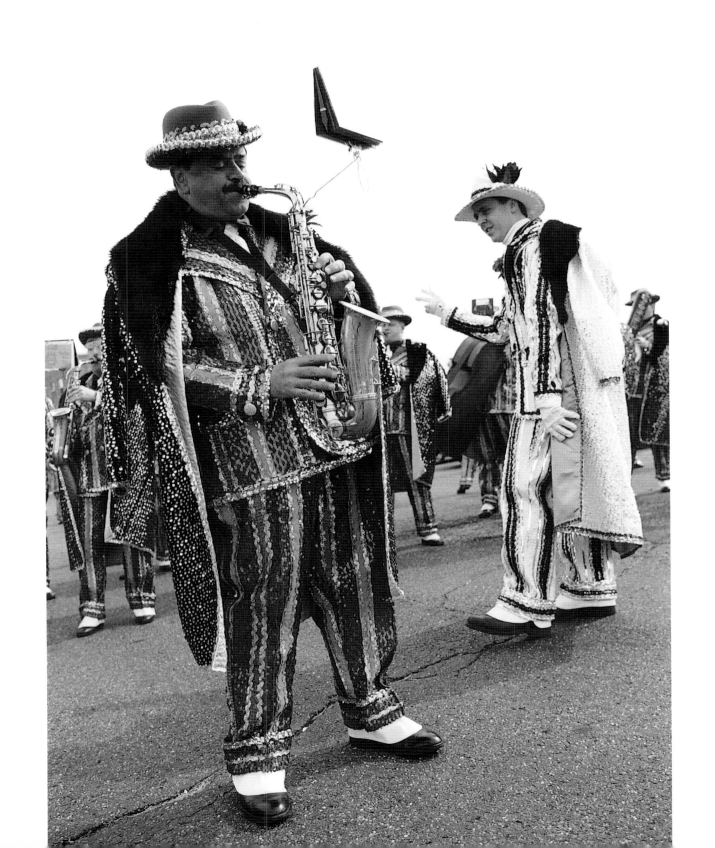

bors' doors for food and drink. The party spilled into the streets, and before long men started donning their wives' dresses and dancing up a winter storm. It was enough fun that in 1901, they applied for a permit and made the party official.

The nation's oldest New Year's party hasn't reached last call yet.

All three of Marty Rotindo's sons—all of them born on November 22—got involved with the Mummers because they saw their father strut.

"When I was three years old I went down to the parade with a toy sax and I mimicked from the street as my father played," Phil recalls. "When I was ten, I was really heavily into the sax, and then I joined Ferko when I was 16."

Those are the rules. Ferko members have to be at least 16. That's when Phil began. That's when Marty Jr. and Nick began, too. "I was watching on TV at home, I was real young," says Marty Jr., now 23. "My father was in a turtle suit, and I said, 'I want to do that some day.'"

Adds Nick, his twin: "We grew up as kids watching him, so we just kind of naturally followed him." Nick is probably the most accomplished musician of the Rotindo family, holding a degree in trombone performance from the Hartt School of Music in Connecticut and currently pursuing his master's degree in music

education at the University of the Arts in Philadelphia.

The problem for him, though, was that Mummers allow only string and reed instruments, and the trombone is a brass instrument. Then again, no problem. He simply picked up the accordion and learned it quickly.

All the Rotindos say their friends think being a Mummer is cooler than anything. They drink a few beers together, go on road trips together, their dancing feet taking them places they otherwise would never visit. In the end, they're guys who just happen to like moving to their own music. And it's not as if the only thing they do is dance and play music. Which, as it happens, is part of the Mummers' charm. Most of the year, they're construction workers, businessmen, lawyers—guys more into sports than sequins.

Marty Sr. is chief financial officer of Larami Limited, the company that makes SuperSoaker water guns. Phil sells advertising for a South Philly newspaper. Marty Jr. is an accountant, and Nick is a music teacher.

"We're pretty sports-oriented," says Marty Jr. of how the Rotindos spend their non-costumed time. "We like to go to Phillies games, Flyers games, pretty much all the sports. But we like to be Mummers, too."

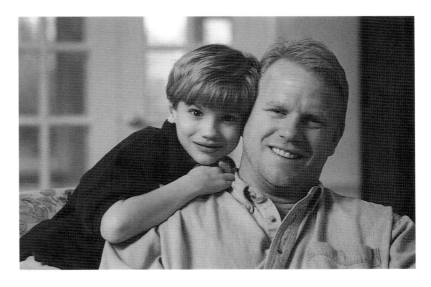

The Esiasons: Boomer and Gunnar

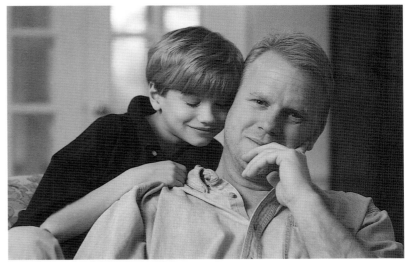

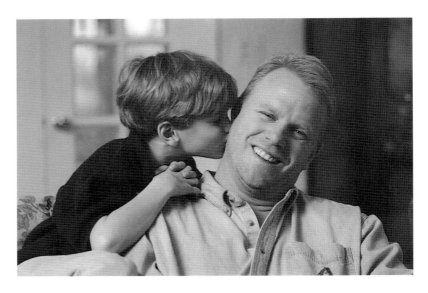

Gunnar Esiason and his dad Boomer.

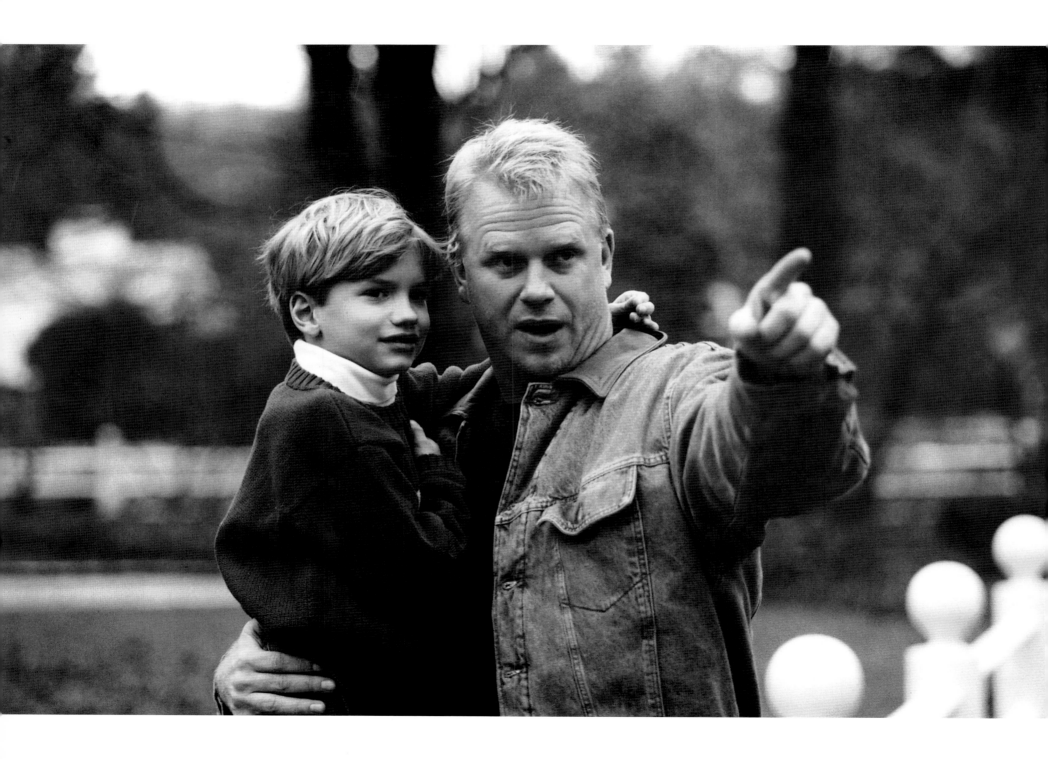

For Boomer Esiason, it was all going as anticipated. He realized his dream to play football in the NFL, he married the perfect woman, and now the plan was to have four daughters, all of them with blond hair and blue eyes and every bit as silly and giggly as blond-haired, blue-eyed little girls can be. Then in 1991 came Gunnar. Not just a son, but all boy.

"My idea of the perfect child changed that day," says Boomer, former announcer for ABC's *Monday Night Football*. "I was like, damn, this is awesome. I'm going to have a little boy to hang out with, someone I can take to ball games, play catch with."

Gunnar and his father go to ball games all right, lots of them, just as planned. And they play catch. The father broadcasts on the radio and the son falls asleep listening to him. They play video games together, watch movies together, and occasionally they go into hysterical fits of laughter together. But for all the good, there is another activity they have to share. Gunnar is one of about 30,000 Americans with cystic fibrosis, a genetic defect that causes the lungs, pancreas, and sweat glands to produce an excess of mucus. So, Boomer Esiason must sharply thump his hands on his son's back, chest, and stomach to expel mucus from his lungs. There also is a nightly regimen that includes aerosol medicines, digestive enzymes, and antibiotics to prevent infections. There have been great advances in treatments, and something resembling promises are on the horizon, but most people with cystic fibrosis do no survive past age 32.

"There's a lot of stress associated with it, of course," says Esiason. "But honestly, when you're around a special-needs child. . . . They are the most fulfilling children to be around. The special things they bring you are unbelievable. When you see them struggle, you have no struggles in life. I've been around a lot of these kids and every one of them has just been special, like they're angels, like they're touched by God."

Esiason was playing quarterback for the Cincinnati Bengals when Gunnar was born. From the beginning, the boy had problems. There were ear infections. His breathing was often labored. "There were a lot of sleepless nights," Esiason says. "I can remember, I would put him in my car and I'd drive him around the beltway in Cincinnati because that's the only way we could get him to sleep. He would sleep sitting up." Doctors examined Gunnar and misdiagnosed him. They ordered cough suppressants when coughing was what the boy needed most.

In 1993, Esiason was traded to the New York Jets. Although his son and his wife, Cheryl—then pregnant with their daughter, Sydney— remained in Cincinnati, training camp on Long Island was just minutes from Boomer's boyhood home, and he was psyched for his first real workout with the team. "I was absolutely ecstatic," he recalls. "It's my first day on the field, and I get an emergency call from my wife. My son was in the hospital having trouble breathing." Esiason bolted back to Cincinnati, where Gunnar, 2 years old, had tubes running into his arms, into his nose.

Doctors ran tests. There was tense waiting. Finally, a pediatric pulmonologist told Esiason and Cheryl that Gunnar had cystic fibrosis. "About two minutes after talking to them I just asked them to leave the room and Cheryl and I just bawled for about forty-five minutes," Esiason, recalls. "Here we are, looking at him, he's sleeping, and he has these tubes in him. . . . You can't imagine the feeling. Since that day, our first mission in life has been to make sure Gunnar is taken care of physically, mentally, emotionally, that he gets love and support and knows he's not in this fight alone. The other thing, just as important, is to make sure Sydney doesn't get lost in this, that she's able to thrive."

Ironically, Esiason had already been involved in raising money for a cure for cystic fibrosis. Six years earlier, he listened to the writer Frank

DeFord give a speech about the death of his daughter, Alex, from the disease, and Esiason decided to help. He became an ambassador for Children's Hospital in Cincinnati. Since his son's diagnosis, he has founded the Boomer Esiason Foundation, which has raised millions of dollars to fight the disease.

Gunnar knows he has cystic fibrosis, but he is 7 and is not aware of the current prognosis for its victims. "We don't tell him, 'Look, you have cystic fibrosis, a fatal genetic disease,'" Esiason says. "We tell him you have the goopies in your lungs. He can comprehend he has a problem. He's not a dummy. We don't need to go farther than that with him yet."

So Gunnar does the things boys do. He plays ice hockey and worships the New York Rangers. He likes whipping his father in Nintendo. ("I usually beat him but I play a lot more," he says.) His favorite subjects in school: "Gym, recess, and science." Smart, pensive, curious, and funny, he tends to fidget when he is asked questions by strangers, but when the subject turns to his father, he opens up, especially when he is asked about "Special Spot Time," as the father and son call it. "Almost every night before I go to bed, we lay down and I put my head on his chest and we watch a little TV," Gunnar says. "I like to be with my daddy and watch TV. I like watching movies with him. He has to cover my eyes for a couple of things I can't see, but it's nice. I've been doing that since I was a baby."

And the favorite thing about Dad? "There's too many good things. I can't pick just one."

Boomer Esiason makes sure his wife hears this when he finds out, later, what his son has said. "Can't pick just one," the father brags. "Did you hear what he said? Can't pick just one."

His daughter, Sydney, is just as the father had dreamed: blond-haired, blue-eyed, silly and giggly and adorable beyond belief. Gunnar, not a dream in the conventional sense, has become a dreamchild in his father's eyes. Boomer is not in denial. He knows the prognosis for his son. "But we can't sit around and believe it's going to be fatal," he says. "We have to hope, and we do have hope. It's an ever-changing world, right?"

For now he will cling to scientific advances, however incremental. More than that, he will cling to moments like this one: He is sitting in a pizza joint near his Long Island home. He grew up in the area, and while he is a celebrity here, to be sure, he is also just a guy sent to pick up his two children from school. Before taking them home, he stops in the restaurant, banters with the locals, and sits with Gunnar, and Sydney, now 5. The children are not eating quickly enough, and Boomer is beginning to lose his patience. But then the kids go into a fit of unstoppable laugher; the father has lost control of them and knows it, and as people in the restaurant look over at his table and slow the pace of their chewing, Boomer Esiason begins to laugh with his children until he too cannot stop.

Maybe it's hokey, but maybe this small point is worth noting: When Boomer was laughing, he did not put a balled hand in front of his mouth the way many men tend to do when they're embarrassed to be laughing so hard, so genuinely with children; he looked right at his kids and laughed with them. Little Sydney laughed so hard she finally snorted through her nose, and—of course—that only made things funnier. And Gunnar? He laughed and laughed and laughed until finally his stomach contractions loosened some of the fluid around his lungs, and he had to catch his breath; but that was difficult, so he just continued to laugh through the coughing.

"Yeah, right," the father finally says a few moments after the laughter subsided. "I got it made." Blessings, it seems, can come unexpectedly.

The Webbs: Marc and Brad

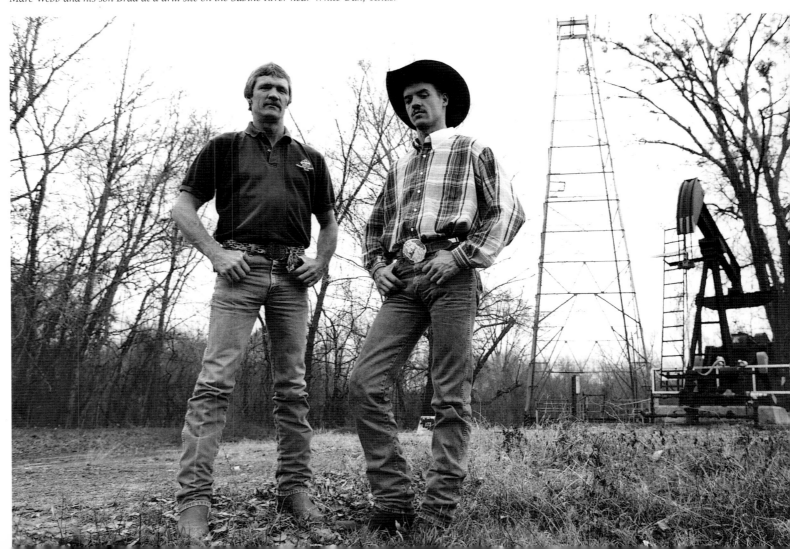

Marc Webb and his son Brad at a drill site on the Sabine River near White Oak, Texas.

For Marc Webb, it was the perfect plan that went awry. When his 16-year-old son, Brad, defiantly announced a few years back that he would no longer attend school, Marc was in a quandary. He had a couple of college classes under his belt and knew the value of education, but neither he nor Brad's mother could talk sense into the boy, couldn't get him to agree to put in just a couple of more years to get that diploma from his Texas high school.

"It was fixing to become a legal problem over truancy, so I went to court and got him pulled out of school and made him work in the oil fields with me," Marc explains. Brad was rustled out of bed at 5:30 in the morning, then worked ten-hour days digging ditches in the oil fields of Eastern Texas for $5.25 an hour in conditions alternating between searing heat and bone-rattling cold.

"I thought he'd be begging to go back to school by the second week," Marc says. "What backfired on me was, no, he wanted to work in the oil fields and make money. He wanted to work in them more than I wanted him to, that's for sure."

Brad, now 21, has worked the fields ever since, in Texas, in Louisiana, and in three other states.

"I had been working summers in the oil fields making $200 to $300 a week, which is a lot of money when you're 15 or 16," Brad explains. "Then I was going to school and not making anything. It got to where I didn't really see a need for school at the time."

At his father's insistence, Brad got his G.E.D. right away. And since his initiation to the fields, he has worked his way up from digging ditches to rigging electrical currents to prevent pipelines from rusting. "I got smart and learned how to run equipment so I didn't have to run the shovels any more," he says.

His father has been in the oil business for twenty-five years, first as a roustabout, now as a foreman overseeing the repair of wells, working for what has become BP Amoco. Webb works for a week near his home in Gladewater, Texas, then works a week in southern Louisiana, home to some of the most productive gas wells in the world. His father worked the fields as well.

Fathers tend to want better lives for their sons than what they had, but oil has been pretty good to the Webb family. So Marc had to walk a fine line when dealing with Brad's insistence to drop out of school and work in the fields. On the one hand, he wanted the boy to have options for his future. That required an education. On the other hand, the fact that he was choosing to follow in his father's footsteps—even without the education—was something Marc didn't want to discourage. "Oh, I guess I'm glad he got into it," the father admits. "I just didn't want him to get into it as early as he did."

And he's glad Brad's working as he is, despite some dangers inherent to laboring in those fields "Those wells have a lot of potential for major blowouts," says Marc, 45. In layman's terms, that means explosions. The wells are drilled about 20,000 feet deep, and the only way to work them is to pump heavy fluid into them. When the gas bubbles up, it rises and expands, and if there's a mistake on gauging just where the gas is, an explosion can occur.

"You get all the right combinations going and what you get is a well that's out of control," Marc explains. "The atmosphere is just full of gas, there are all these engines running and all you need is one spark . . ."

Only a few years ago, a well Marc was working on went out of control just across the state line in northern Louisiana. With no safety equipment in place, natural gas shot 150 feet into the air, just searching for a spark to ignite it. "Fortunately," Marc says, "we got away without a fire."

The Webbs' hometown of Gladewater boomed after oil was discovered under its dusty land in 1931, the population increasing from 500 to about 10,000. Even though a dry spell for the oil industry put many of the town's businesses under in the mid-1980s, all along Texas Route 80, which splits the town in two, oil-pumping units still churn on the side of the road. A ways further, toward Kilgore, the old oil derricks still provide the skyline with a rustic elegance that speaks of grand Depression-era dreams of wealth, some of them realized, some of them not.

Since the boom busted, not much else has moved into town aside from antique shops, leaving young men like Brad to choose between working at McDonald's or working the oil fields. For Brad, the choice was easy, even if it did come too soon.

"There's nothing I like about it," he says. "It's all about the money. You burn up in the summer and freeze in the winter." But then he gets to thinking about his job, about the long days that are never quite alike, about the travel, and about being outdoors, and his tune changes. "I stay in one place for two or three days, tops, then I move on. It's not like going to an office and sitting at the same desk every day. It's like there's more freedom."

If there's anything more important to Texans than freedom, it's oil. The combination of the two—and the money the job would bring—was enough to convince Brad that school wasn't for him. Up until then, he and his father had a close relationship, going out fishing on their boat, Marc coaching Brad in soccer. But once Brad got his driver's license and a bit of money in his pocket from working in the fields, things began to change.

He spent his money on accessories for his pickup truck, on giant belt buckles and cowboy boots and cowboy hats, and all other things that a kid from rural Texas wants to own.

"He had a hunger for money," his father says. "When he made up his mind he wanted something, he wanted it."

So he quit going to school. And while that move caused a good amount of friction between him and his father at the time, something about the whole dropping-out ordeal has worked to their advantage these days.

"He told me I'd regret dropping out, and now I do," Brad says. "If I had to do it over again, I'd go back. But I can't." In the past few years, that's partly what convinced him that his father was worth not just talking to, but listening to as well. And when classes are offered by the company he's working for now, Brad takes them.

"It's like as I've gotten older, it's turned into more of a friendship than a father–son thing," Brad says. "Now I can come over and talk to him about different stuff, stuff I wouldn't have when I was a kid. When I was a kid, I didn't see it, but now that I've gotten older I can see he's been there, done that. It's like he can tell me what's going to happen later in my life. It's kind of like getting my fortune told."

"Oh," replies Marc, "I tell him what I want him to believe. It may not be true, but I tell him what I think he should hear. That's what daddy's do."

The Graves: Henry, Adam, and Mark

Henry Graves sits in the backyard of his home in Ontario, Canada, and clicks through his kids: There is son Adam, star of the National Hockey League's New York Rangers. There are Richenda and Lynette, the daughters he adores. So far a very nuclear family. But then there is the boy who picks through the garbage when he gets hungry; there is the one who refuses to talk, ever; there is the violent one, who once pulled a knife; there are older kids and infants, healthy kids and ones who are damaged, some psychologically, some physically, some both; and there is the one obsessed with mowing the lawn, insisting that he cut the grass even when it's far from due.

"Oh, that one, he's psychotic," Henry says, a big grin taking over his face. "I just love him."

For Henry and his wife, Lynda, and for Adam and his sisters, these other kids needed help, and so they got it. Adam would clear the top bunk for new "brothers," Richenda and Lynette would make room for new "sisters," all of them among the more than

From left, Henry, Mark, and Adam Graves outside their Ontario home.

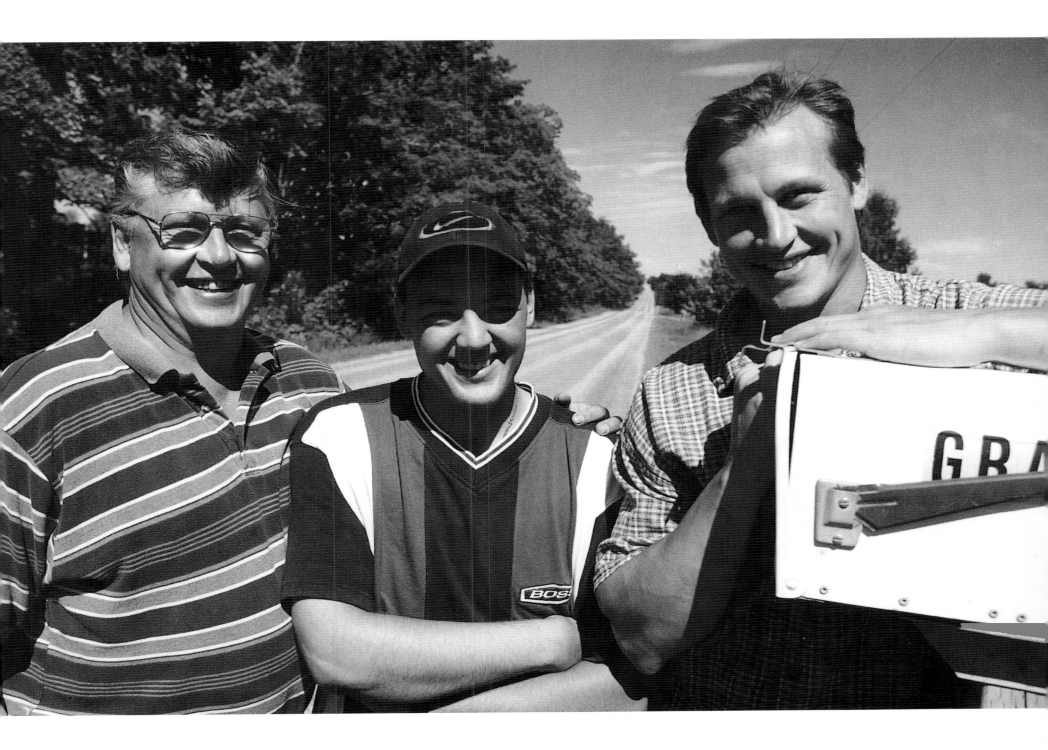

forty foster children Henry and Lynda have taken in over the years. They took in a lot of emergency kids, accepting a lot of late-night/early morning calls from social service workers in Canada looking to house someone in the Graves's home—some for days, some for years. One of them, Mark, they kept.

"It wasn't anything out of the ordinary," Adam says, looking back on his childhood. "That was part of life. For us, the biggest compliment we could get was when they considered us brothers and sisters, and for Mum and Dad, it was when the kids called them Mum and Dad."

For Adam, the new brothers never threatened the bond he forged with his father, a retired Toronto police officer—a "copper" as he calls himself—and a big kid himself, really. Helping kids in trouble was just another part of life they've shared over the years, along with hockey in the driveway and water fights in the yard and the kind of ribbing that goes on between fathers and sons who thoroughly enjoy each other's company. The same goes for Mark, the shy one in the family, who listens to his father and Adam tell stories, chirping in occasionally but preferring to sit back and laugh, obviously happy, which shouldn't be a great surprise. It's not every guy, after all, who gets to choose his family.

Mark came to the Graves when he was 4 and Adam was 13. As with most of the foster kids, Adam bonded with him, never jealous that he had to share his parents' attention. The affection they have for each other is unabashed. ("Remember that one, eh?" Adam says to Mark with a laugh at every story that bubbles to the surface.) Mark was clearly one of the special ones the Graves took in. As he started getting older, though, social workers told Henry and Lynda that he was reaching the age where he'd no longer be adoptable. The couple reached a decision: "When he was old enough to understand what adoption was," Lynda recalls, "we told him he could adopt us if he wanted to."

"The biggest memory I have of it was the name," says Mark. "I said, 'I'd like you to be my parents, can I have your name, too?'" They gave him the name, a home, and a family. Now, more than fifteen years later, on their patio in Erin, about forty-five minutes outside of Toronto, the family gets to telling stories and there is no stopping them. Henry punctuates every memory with a laugh. He roars at "The Henry Olympics," a family contest of different events from miniature golf to volleyball, basketball, and, of course, road hockey. Henry brags that he won the go-kart portion of the "competition," raising his arms in triumph even as he concedes he was booted from the track for some questionable driving practices.

"He paid for it, though," says Adam. "He got cocky. After that we went to the batting cages and he broke his thumb." And it was the team of Adam, Mark, and Augie—the brother of Adam's wife Violet—that won the overall competition. Adam recalls it like his father, arms pumping above his head, hands balled into fists.

Henry is quick to respond: "But who won the hockey portion?" He reaches into the air as if he's pulling the lever of a slot machine. "Whoo-Whoo!"

Henry, as far as anyone in the family can recall, has always been this way. When Adam was growing up, the neighborhood kids would come to their home looking to scare up a hockey game. Always, they asked for Adam *and* his father. When a water fight broke out, Henry, not content with how things were going, climbed on his roof and soaked everyone from up there. And for two hours a day, Henry stood in front of a goalie's net at the end of the driveway, while Adam fired shots at him. They did it from the time Adam was about 5 until he was 12. "Every year he'd have to go back a little further or I would've gotten killed," Henry recalls. "He went back further and further until he finally got to the street, and

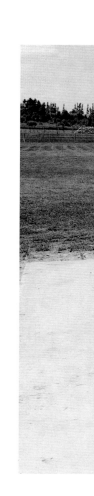

then I said, 'Okay, it's time we don't have a goalie. We just shoot.'"

More than the lessons on how to skirt the rules in go-kart racing or how best to soak someone in a water fight, the time spent shooting pucks paid off. Adam was a first-round pick for the Canadian Junior A team when he was 16. In the NHL, he paid his dues with the Detroit Red Wings from 1987 to 1989, then was dealt to the Edmonton Oilers, where he promptly helped them win the 1989–1990 Stanley Cup. In 1991, he signed with the New York Rangers and has been an All-Star, breaking a Rangers scoring record—fifty-one goals in a season—that

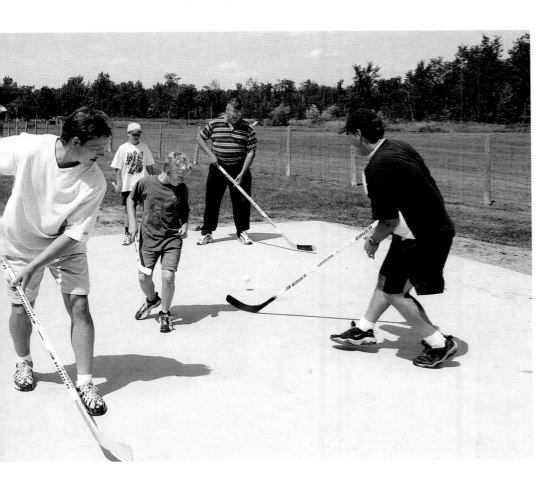

had stood for twenty-two years. He was part of the Ranger team that won the Stanley Cup in 1994.

His father, of course, is proud of those accomplishments. But he's more proud of his son's off-the-ice goals, the ones he has scored for the benefit of others. Like his father, Adam gives a particularly large portion of his time to children. He works with drug rehabilitation groups, with the Ronald McDonald House, and with inner-city youth. Even during the season, he travels to Brooklyn to read *Curious George* books to kids from Family Dynamics, a New York City agency that strengthens homes by providing support and counseling to children and parents.

"Your mark when you leave this world is not how many goals you've scored but how many people you've helped achieve their goals," says Henry. "The hockey's great but what I'm really proud of is the nature and character of my son and the man he's developed into."

"Whoa!" Adam interrupts. "I guess I'm buying dinner tonight." He is serious, though, when he talks of why he spends so much time with charity work. "I was fortunate to grow up in an atmosphere and a family setting that not everyone is fortunate enough to grow up in. All the kids that came through this house, and the way my mum and dad worked with them, I saw that to be a strong person—not on the ice but in life—you get most of that from your family."

Mark is proof of that philosophy. When he first got to the Graves' house he was a handful. The details of the problems he was having—and causing—aren't important now. Suffice it to say he was troubled. Now 21, he works, hard, as maintenance man, is unfailingly polite, and revels in his family.

"I was pretty lucky," he says. "I got a family that has always stuck with me and helped me through some of the harder times. For them it's always been about family, and now it's the same for me."

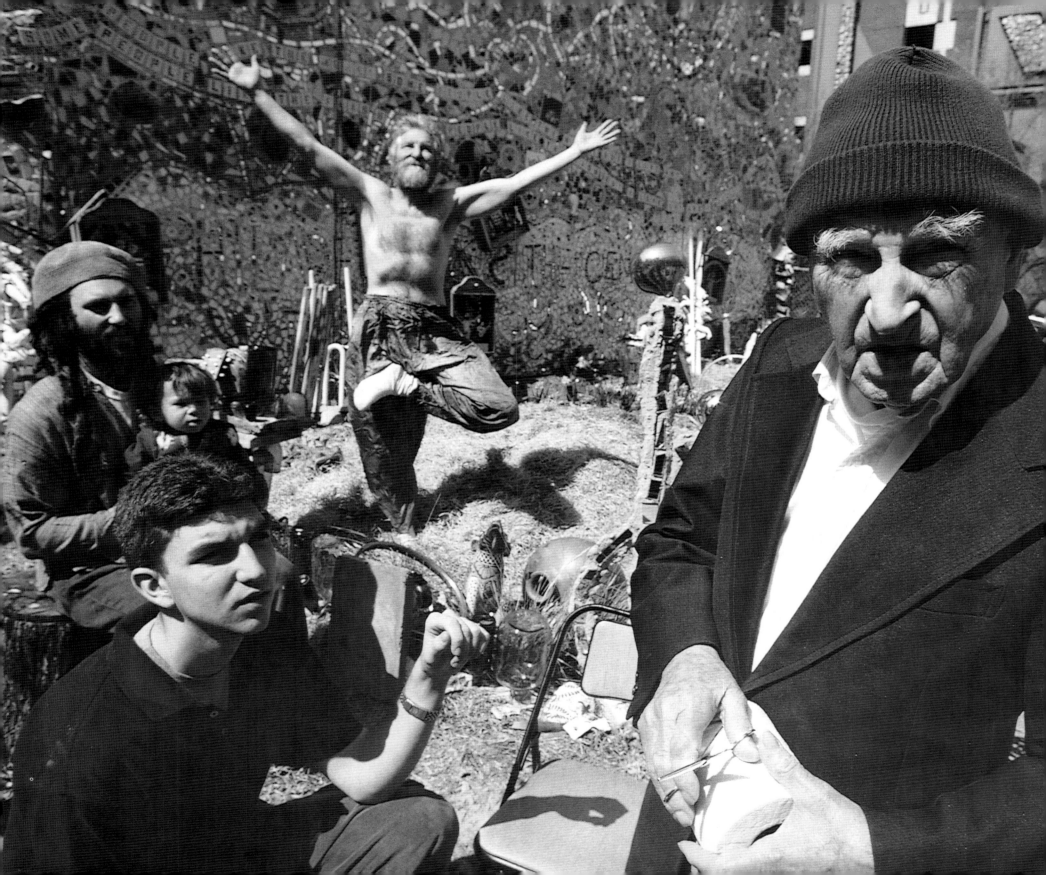

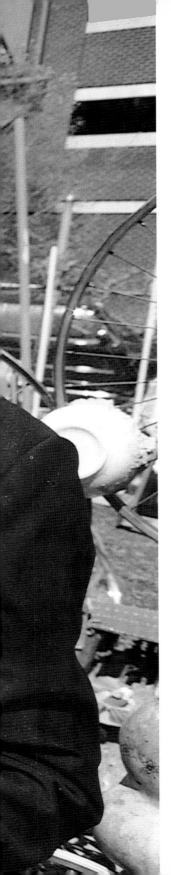

The Zagars: Asher, Isaiah, Ezekiel, Jeremiah, and Yoel

sher Zagar counts his pennies one by one, sizing them up through wild, falling eyebrows and then pushing them into piles with old, crooked fingers. Then he counts them again and again still. He will put them aside for a second or two for something important, but it has to be something very important, and he will insist that those pennies remain close by. He sleeps with them. The old man is also fond of models in magazines, but he pities those models, too. That is clear from the conversations he has with them. "Why do you look so unhappy?" he asks one staring back at him from the page. She is a model in *Playboy*.

And so it goes. Asher counts his pennies, then he talks to his models, and his mind moves along in its own way. It is not so much the coins and the women that are important to him; it's the repetition. For a man who can get lost in his own house, change is frightening, repetition is not. So he values it like air. Another constant is his attempt to find his parents. The pennies go in his pockets, the models are placed on a coffee

Clockwise from right, Asher, Jeremiah, Ezekial, holding his son Yoel, and Isaiah Zagar among Isaiah's artwork.

table, and the search begins. He shuffles, pulls a black knit cap over his hair, wispy and gray, and then he stretches that cap farther down, over his big, rubbery ears. He loves his parents. He searches for them often, though he is in his nineties and they are long since dead. He knew that once. But now. . . . He looks for them around the hallways in his house, around the corners of his street. His habits charm his family in some ways. But those habits, his family knows, are indications that his mind is fading away, permanently.

"He still recognizes me," says his son, Isaiah, an artist. "But there will come a day when he won't."

"Hey, Daddy!" The son speaks loudly to his father, who is only a foot away. "We're going to be in a book, Daddy! We have to pose naked! You can wear your shoes, though! Shoes are okay!"

"I always wear my shoes," the father replies, and a smile seeps out of him, but he is not in on the joke.

Humor is one way the family deals with Asher's Alzheimer's disease. Isaiah, now in his sixties himself, is sure of the diagnosis, although it is not official. "What would be the point?" Isaiah asks. "Medication isn't what he needs. There's nothing they can do for him. Attention is what he needs."

Since 1991, Asher and Isaiah Zagar have lived together in a townhouse on Philadelphia's South Street. That year Asher Zagar's wife—Isaiah's mother—was diagnosed with brain cancer. She and Asher moved in with their son and his wife, Julia.

"We set up a room as a hospice," Isaiah says. "She died in that room. He carried on, and until about four years ago he was pretty independent. Now he's not. We had some hairy moments until we figured out how to keep him locked in the house during the day. He was always escaping, looking for his parents, and he'd always find a way to get out.

For him, his parents live in a parallel universe. They live in the same building, but somewhere else, and for some reason he looked for them outside. Now, we take him around the block and he's happy to get home. His parents are here somewhere."

"Would you like some orange juice, Daddy?!" Isaiah asks.

"It's good orange juice," the father replies.

When Asher Zagar's mind was complete, it was precise and brilliant. He was an electrical and mechanical engineer, well schooled and devout in his Judaism, good with the earliest of computers, and with a penchant and a talent for photography. "That's when he had all his marbles," the son says in front of his father. There is no cruelty in the comment, nor a hint of sadness. It is just the way things are. Blunt talk is another way the family deals with Asher's disease. ("Being with my father for a whole day is devastating," Isaiah says. "It doesn't have the reward of bringing up children and seeing them into another part of their life. It's bringing a person slowly but surely to death.") For Isaiah, the pain of watching a brilliant mind fade is channeled into his artwork. He takes the pain of his father's plight and mixes it with the joy he finds in his own sons, Ezekiel and Jeremiah, and in his grandson, Yoel, now a toddler.

Isaiah Zagar's art comes in the form of mosaics. His pieces are an assemblage of disparate parts in all colors of glass, mirrors, ceramics, or drawings and photographs encased in glass. They are three-dimensional, covering the insides of houses, apartments, and offices—in kitchens, bathrooms, and stairwells, on the floors, walls, and ceilings. Outdoors, the art is bricks, reenforcing rods and mortar embellished with bottles, broken crockery, and other sculptural components. Much of what he uses is folk art that has been sent to the studio he and his wife run in Philadelphia. The artwork that arrives broken, he

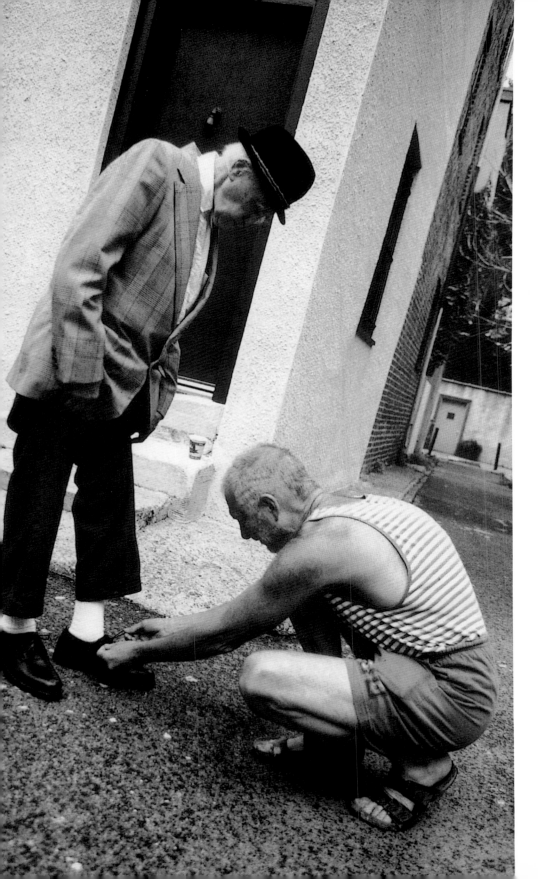

simply incorporates into his mosaics. More often than not, the Zagar family runs through Isaiah's work: Within the mosaics he will form the name of his father, his sons, his grandson, and he will often encase their pictures in the art.

"He's always put his family in his artwork," says 30-year-old Ezekiel, his elder son, now a father himself. "The strain of his father hasn't been easy—it's been kind of exhausting—but I think he uses it, I think that's true. Now, he gets some energy taking a lot of pictures of my son. His artwork has always been like that, though. He takes pictures, does drawings, puts the names of people he loves in the tiles. In a way, it's simple, straightforward, not really anything too sublime in its individual parts. Yet it's very sublime in the whole. He might not agree with me, or wouldn't say it that way, but I see how people react to it. They say, 'Ah, it makes me happy.' They don't understand that the names they're reading are names in my father's life, but it makes them feel good. It's on a subliminal level."

"I don't know exactly how to explain it . . ." Isaiah struggles. "In a sense, I try to utilize the terrifying aspects of what he has become into some malevolent spirit for my work to thrive on. I've done a lot of art objects about my father and artwork relating to him. Then there's another side. I took my father to the studio with me. He's a counter of pennies, but he's also good at the repetition of putting tiles one next to the other. He did that for me, and filled two full tables, and then I painted on those tiles. You could say, 'This poor guy, all he can do is count pennies all day,' but you know what? He can fill a table with tiles. And I need those tiles, and I can thank him for that."

Jeremiah, Isaiah's younger son, is 17 and still lives at home. So he has seen firsthand his father's dealings with his grandfather, Asher, has taken care of his grandfather himself. Although barely starting in life, his grandfather's experience has given him the perspective of an older man.